ST

CHILDREN

*The tragedy and challenge of the world's
millions of modern-day Oliver Twists.*

STREET CHILDREN

The tragedy and challenge of the world's
millions of modern-day Oliver Twists.

Andy Butcher

NELSON WORD PUBLISHING

STREET CHILDREN

Published by Nelson Word Ltd., Milton Keynes, England.

ISBN 1-86024-028-3

Scripture quotations are from the Holy Bible, New International Version, © 1973, 1978, 1984 by International Bible Society.

British Library Cataloguing in Publication Data. A catalogue record for this book is available from the British Library.

Reproduced, printed and bound in Great Britain for Nelson Word Ltd. by Cox & Wyman Ltd., Reading.

96 97 98 / 10 9 8 7 6 5 4 3 2 1

To Matthew, Samuel, Hannah and Daniel

*May you always be sure of your
'rightful inheritance': the love
and security that is yours in two
homes—one temporarily and
imperfectly here on earth, the
other eternally and perfectly
in heaven.*

CONTENTS

FOREWORD BY STEVE CHALKE

Last Christmas I received a card from a Christian friend that simply read, 'Jesus, born in a stable'. But the truth is that none of the Gospels mention a stable. It is just another one of those little add-ons we have made. The traditional picture of Jesus' birth is about as far from reality as it is possible to get.

The Christmas story, as we all know, is filled with distortions of the truth, based not on the Bible's down-to-earth account of how things *actually* were, but on the sentiment and soft focus of popular mythology. But the biggest distortion of all is not the one about baby not crying, or the cows not mooing, or there being three kings, or Jesus being born on December 25th. It's something even more basic.

Luke, for instance, records that Mary and Joseph were in Bethlehem for a census, and that whilst they were there, Mary gave birth to her firstborn—a son. He then explains that they had to make do with a manger—an animal feeding trough—because there was no room for mother and baby at the local inn. We are not told, incidentally, whether the manger was in a stable, outside the front entrance to the inn, or somewhere totally different.

What we *do* know from Luke's account is that Joseph only managed to find somewhere for his young bride and her new born son *after* Jesus had been born. And because he was poor and Bethlehem was crowded, the best he could find was the feeding trough. So there is a very strong probability that Jesus was actually born on the street: in the gutter or in a secluded corner, wherever Joseph could find Mary a semi-private place to squat. All this is not for the squeamish. And it's about as far from the glitzy and glamorous version of the Christmas story as you can get. But it *is* the truth.

The issue of the world's millions of street children is one that should be right at the centre of our Christian concern. Why? Because when God became a human being, he did not become just any human being. He became a specific human being. He chose to be born into poverty. He became a child who began life on the streets. In other words, Jesus, the Saviour of the World, was a street child.

I am pleased to endorse this book. Not because it is well written, dealing in an accessible, informative and gripping style with an issue that every responsible Christian must be concerned about. But also because, rather than merely seeking to analyse the situation, its goal is to make a difference. God's way of dealing with suffering was, and is, to get involved. That is what the Christmas story is all about. And reading this book will inspire you to take action.

But there is even more to it than that. Today, the *Oasis Trust* is working amongst street children in a number of countries around the world, including India. And in India's biggest city, Bombay, we have developed several projects which aim to meet their spiritual and material needs with everything from housing and medical care, education and employment, to the love and security they deserve. I am very grateful to Andy Butcher, to Nelson Word and to you, because a percentage from the sale of every copy of this book will go towards the development of our work with some of the hundreds of thousands of children in such desperate need in that city.

Steve Chalke, Oasis Trust
London, December 1995

ACKNOWLEDGEMENTS

A S A LONG-TIME CINEMA LOVER, I have always wondered why they insist on putting the credits on at the end of the film. Given that most people scramble for the cinema exit doors or reach for the VCR hand control the minute the action stops, it leaves a lot unsaid. Viewers can be forgiven for going away with the idea that what they have seen was really all about just the handful of names that went up in lights before the feature began. They forget that an awful lot of work went on behind the scenes to give others the platform for a starring role.

So it is nice to be able to reverse cinematic wisdom, and give credit where it is due: right up front, before it all begins. This book may have my name on the cover, but it is only there because of the efforts of many others.

First and foremost my priceless wife, Amanda, who has shared with me a concern about the issue of street children for the past several years. She was a constant source of encouragement and constructive criticism as the project developed. And she many times cheerfully shouldered extra responsibilities at home to allow me the time needed to travel, research and write.

Without her the book would simply have remained only an idea.

Our children—Matthew, Samuel, Hannah and Daniel—also gave up Dad Time graciously for the homeless kids they prayed for on many occasions.

Noel Halsey, in England, is to be thanked for his enthusiasm for and commitment to the project from its first suggestion, and for his great patience in seeing it come to fruition. Linda Finley-Day played a key part, too, in helping shape the final result.

Many of our church family at New Malden Baptist, in England, together with a chain of friends across the world, prayed for us faithfully through the many months it took to complete.

Paul McCusker was both a good friend and a critical eye at the right time, and Paul Daw brought some very special words of encouragement just when they were needed. Thank you!

Too numerous to name individually are the many people who agreed to be interviewed at length, or gave freely of their expertise or their archives and other resources.

To everyone who offered comments, experiences, documents and reports, my sincere thanks. Wherever possible they have been credited in the text, or notes.

However I must mention Johan and Jeanette Lukasse in Belo Horizonte, Brazil, Danny Smith and the Jubilee team in Surrey, England, and Jeff Anderson and his ACTION colleagues in Manila, the Philippines, for their particular open-handedness and help.

Events and quotes are as they were observed and recorded during my interviews and visits, unless otherwise referenced.

Finally Beth Johnson and her husband Jan generously provided a wonderful writer's mountain retreat at a critical stage of drafting this manuscript, helping the words along no end.

Any good or lasting value that may come from the following pages, I am more than happy to share with all those named above.

Any weaknesses, shortcomings or other faults are all just mine.

Andy Butcher
Colorado Springs, November 1994

INTRODUCTION

A STOLEN INHERITANCE . . .

'Please sir, I want some more.'

OLIVER TWIST: CHAPTER TWO

THEY ARE AMONG the six most famous words of childhood.

Angel-faced, tousle-haired, the young boy holds out his bowl in innocent appeal and asks for a second helping to fill his empty stomach.

'Please sir, I want some more.'

The simple plea has tugged at countless hearts through the years, as it has been made on the stage and the screen, in song and cartoon animation.

Charles Dickens' classic story of the workhouse boy who runs away to London only to fall into the wrong hands is known and loved the world over. At least, superficially.

For the popular versions actually do Oliver—and his many, real-life 'descendants' on the streets of cities around the world today, as you read—a great injustice.

The chances are that the adaptation you remember brings back warm, fluffy feelings of angels with dirty faces. Victorian predecessors of Dennis the Menace, all innocent mischief and harmless pranks.

But Dickens' original work, for all its happy-ever-after

naïveté, is much darker, a different matter to the average twentieth-century interpretation.

Read backlit by shadowy 1800s London streetlights rather than glossy present-day neon, the likes of Fagin, Bill Sykes and the Artful Dodger take on a much more sinister countenance.

For this is no fairy tale. Rather it is a graphic account of some of the world's first street children—complete with violence and abuse, if only you dare to glimpse between the lines.

As such, flickers of the familiar figure of Oliver Twist can be seen on the streets of hundreds, even thousands of cities around the world today.

They sleep in the graveyards of Khartoum, Sudan. On top of bus shelters in Sao Paolo, Brazil. In the sewers of Bogota, Colombia. Behind cardboard in London, England. Under abandoned cars in New York, USA.

They clean shoes in Manila, the Philippines. Steal purses in Milan, Italy. Guard parked cars in Nairobi, Kenya. Sell their bodies in Sydney, Australia. Anything to make enough for something to eat.

And their lives echo Oliver's plea for rather more than he has been served with.

'Please sir, can I have some more?'

More than the meagre portions that leave them constantly hungry, that recruit for sex, drugs, robbery—anything that will kill the pangs or fill the plate.

More than the indifference of adults who only express interest when they get in the way.

More than the prospect of early death from injury or illness.

More than the fear of ending up in jail after tangling with the police, or in the local morgue after running foul of one of the death squads.

Closer reading of Oliver's original story reveals that his request was not simply a matter of youthful greed, or even childish need.

It was also a question of justice.

For as his would-be benefactor investigates, he discovers that Oliver is not just a workhouse orphan.

Although illegitimate, it turns out that Oliver's father is a wealthy businessman—and that the villain Fagin and his cronies are determined to prevent him from receiving his due inheritance.

For Oliver, there was a happy conclusion. But a century and a half later, for many of his modern-day 'offspring' the future does not seem so good. No neat conclusions.

In bus shelters and derelict buildings, on pavements and railway stations, they, too, are being denied an inheritance that is rightly theirs.

The right to nurture and nourishment, help and hope, a family and a future.

These modern-day Olivers are being educationally dis-advantaged. Emotionally wounded. Financially defrauded. Physically abused. Nutritionally starved. Sexually used. Environmentally deprived. Socially rejected. Spiritually scarred.

Young hands hold out begging bowls, glue-sniffing tins, hypodermic needles, weapons.

And the unspoken plea is: 'Please sir, I want some more.'

THREE CITIES, THREE SUMMITS

*'... half-starved ...
cuffed and buffeted through the world,
despised by all and pitied by none.'*

OLIVER TWIST: CHAPTER ONE

Brazil: The Gang and The Gun

I WAS TWENTY-FOUR hours too late to meet **Chico**. The faint stains of his blood were the only mark that he had left behind on the Brazilian streets that had been his home for most of his sixteen or so years.

If you don't count the unborn child being carried by his early-teens girlfriend.

She stood a few dozen yards away from where he had been gunned down, crying silently while other members of the gang hovered around.

Some looked awkwardly at the ground, shifting from foot to foot, while others flicked their eyes menacingly at everyone who passed by, daring someone to start something.

Less than a day after their leader's body had been taken away, Chico's gang were still jumpy. The tension was caught by those arriving at the cinema whose steps and entrance the youngsters considered home. They moved inside briskly.

17

Almost everyone knew him in the neighbourhood around Belo Horizonte's Cine Teato Brasil, on the Rua dos Carijos. He got his nickname Doido—it means 'Crazy' in Portuguese—from the times he would fight wild, or space out on whatever he could sniff or swallow.

And yet he was well-liked by the twenty or so other kids that ran with the gang. He had even been a representative to one of the groups speaking out on the needs of the country's street children.

And then came the evening someone got even.

Chico would go to restaurants and cafés, eat and drink and then refuse to pay, as a taunt. He tried it once too often, pushed once too far.

Infuriated by Chico's cheek, a waiter at one restaurant came up behind him and shot him in the back of the head.

Manila: The Razor's Edge

Nicky sat in the middle of the Manila pavement and tried not to flinch too much as his friend Reinaldo knelt behind him and scraped the razor blade across Nicky's head.

Dabbing the blade occasionally into a plastic cup of dirty water, to wash away the flecks of blood and lubricate the dulled edge, Reinaldo scratched away Nicky's hair like a clumsy hairdresser.

Gradually Nicky's mop fell away to reveal his scalp and the reason for the cropping—cuts and welts across the top of his skull from a fight the previous night in which Nicky had been the loser.

Though caked dry, the wounds were deep enough to warrant stitches. But that would mean a visit to the hospital which would have to be paid for. And the injured twelve-year-old just didn't have that kind of money.

So, instead, Reinaldo offered the standard first aid of the street; shave away the matted hair so that the wounds don't get infected, then sprinkle powdered aspirin over the top as a crude protection.

Arms resting on upturned knees, Nicky cried out a couple of times as Reinaldo's untrained hand and the blunt blade combined to add to the pattern of cuts.

The boys squatted, oblivious to the crowds around in the street behind one of the Philippine capital's busy shopping districts.

But the ragged-clothed youngsters were spotted by a group of students clutching shopping bags who stepped into their path from between two parked cars.

Seeing the boys in front of them, the group turned to their right and, like the priest and the Levite in the parable of the Good Samaritan, swiftly crossed to the other side.

Hollywood: The Dark Side

As he showed me round his neighbourhood, **Tony** recalled how when his mother and stepfather decided that things would work out better without him in the way, they bought Tony a one-way ticket to the other side of the country.

He was thirteen years old.

Ignoring their farewell piece of parental advice—'Don't go

there, it's a crazy place'—he made his way to Los Angeles with a few dollars and even less plans.

Soon he was just another young face on the Hollywood Boulevard, making a few dollars whatever way he could to pay for some cheap booze or drugs.

Together with other members of his punk street gang—mohawk-haired, heavy black make-up—he'd charge tourists to take his photo outside Mann's famous Chinese cinema. A soon-to-be-forgotten kid snapped near the pavements in which the film industry's greats leave their permanent prints.

If the picture pitch was slow, there was always posing as a homosexual prostitute to mug would-be clients, and straightforward shoplifting.

Home was an empty room in a derelict apartment building back up the less glitzy end of the Boulevard. Furnishings: an old crate, dirty mattress and soiled blankets. There he and his buddies would 'do drugs, sex, party . . .'

Handwriting scrawled across the walls testified to another dabble-with-danger for the hundreds of young people like Tony who drift into Hollywood, only to get sucked into its undertow of occultism and perversion.

The words were daubed in blood.

Three cities. Three boys. Three blood stains.

Three first-person snapshots from one terrible reality that is there around the clock, around the globe—streets filled with children trying to make it on their own in an indifferent or hostile world.

It is hard to know which is the worst.

There are many more shocking stories to be told. Countless ugly reports in the files of advocates, welfare bodies, charities, church groups, human rights organisations, and government agencies.

Chico, Nicky and Tony were simply three lives I came into direct contact with as, briefly visiting different parts of the world, I turned the corner into the streets of the children.

The following pages are not an exhaustive study. They do not pretend to have all the answers.

But they hope to ask some of the questions.

Chief among them being to echo Oliver Twist's words on behalf of those following in his bare footsteps.

'Don't they deserve some more?'

There are some who not only believe that they do, but who are attempting to do something about it.

Three 'summits'—in markedly different places—challenge us as Christians to be involved, too.

One took place before the world's media. Another in a private gathering of like-minded people. The third among a group of friends.

Together they make a compelling call to respond to the cries of the young ones who deserve more than they have.

CHAPTER TWO

SAVING TREES, DYING CHILDREN

' "Where does he live?"
"Where he can, your worship,"
replied the officer.'

OLIVER TWIST: CHAPTER ELEVEN

The World Summit for Children

IT WAS THE largest meeting of world leaders in history.
More than seventy of them gathered in New York for two
days in late September 1990 with just one item on the
agenda: children.

From Albania to Zimbabwe, they congregated at the United
Nations headquarters, their ranks including forty-one presi-
dents, twenty-nine prime ministers, a king, a grand duke and
a cardinal.

'The children of the world are innocent, vulnerable and
dependent. They are also curious, active and full of hope,' they
declared.[1]

'Their time should be one of joy and peace, of playing,
learning and growing. Their future should be shaped in har-
mony and cooperation . . .

23

'But for many children, the reality of childhood is altogether different.'

They might have been referring to **Wilson**, out on the streets of **Bogota, Colombia** until almost midnight. His shanty-home parents could not make ends meet so they sent him out to beg alone. He was not allowed to go home until he had netted a dollar, and some days that seemed to take for ever. He cried a lot.[2]

Some of the bigger boys in the area turned their tears off with the help of Boxer, a cleaning fluid that shot them high and dampened the hunger pangs.

Or **Sonia** in **Belo Horizonte, Brazil**. She was just three when she was sent out to beg for the first time. When her father was jailed she was taken to an aunt's house, but left to fend for herself.[3]

Eventually she was picked up by the authorities and taken to an orphanage, but the other girls picked on her and tormented her. Life on the streets seemed better, so she ran away. She was taken in by a gang, and things seemed to be looking up.

Until the night the boys decided she should be initiated. Twelve of them gang-raped her. And again the next night.

Or thirteen-year-old **Joe**, who ran away from his home in **the Midlands, England,** after his mother and stepfather told him they didn't want him any more.[4]

He slept in the park during the summer time, and then found temporary shelter with friends or in unlocked garages when the nights grew cold.

He survived this way for two years, before eventually being

directed to a special children's shelter. During all his time out on his own, he had never been reported missing.

If not these, than any of thousands—even millions—of other tragic stories could have prompted those at the World Summit for Children to recognise:

Each day, countless children around the world are exposed to dangers that hamper their growth and development.

They suffer immensely as casualties of war and violence; as victims of racial discrimination, apartheid, aggression, foreign occupation and annexation; as refugees and displaced children, forced to abandon their homes and their roots; as disabled; or as victims of neglect, cruelty and exploitation.[5]

On the second day of the international forum, they announced a Plan of Action for the 1990s intended to place children 'high and firmly on the agenda . . . giving them priority—or "first call" on the world's resources in good times or bad, war or peace'.[6]

The United Nations Children's Fund (UNICEF), who hosted the event, noted that the unprecedented world forum came at a time of 'great changes', when

the decline in superpower confrontation could mean that, for the first time in more than half a century, nations will be able to turn from hostilities to concentrating on making the world a better place to live.

Such a 'peace dividend' could provide a major impetus for efforts to save the lives of millions of children.[7]

According to UNICEF executive director James Grant,

two-thirds of the 40,000 children dying in the world each day—from preventable diseases and diarrhoea—could be saved with the technology and expertise already available.

'Thousands of deaths . . . take place because the children don't have a dollar's worth of vaccine or because the parents don't know how to make a simple sugar-saltwater solution to combat dehydration,' he said.[8]

Tackling what he called 'the do-able' comprised part of the ambitious goals agreed upon for the coming decade by participants. They included:

- a reduction of under-five child deaths by one third

- halving the maternal mortality rate

- universal access to safe drinking water, and proper sewage facilities

. The summit also committed itself to more wide-ranging issues, including:

- universal access to basic education, with 80 per cent of primary school-aged children completing their studies

- the protection of children in especially difficult circumstances.

This last aim made specific reference to the needs of street children.

'Millions of children around the world live under especially difficult circumstances,' noted the leaders' eleven-page summary:

> ... as orphans and street children, as refugees or displaced persons, as victims of war and natural and man-made disasters, including such perils as exposure to radiation and dangerous chemicals, as children of migrant workers and other socially disadvantaged groups, as child workers or youth trapped in the bond-age of exploitation, as disabled children and juvenile delinquents and as victims of apartheid and foreign occupation.
>
> Such children deserve special attention, protection and assistance from their families and communities and as part of national efforts and international cooperation.[9]

The New York gathering prompted worldwide concern. Television and radio reports, newspaper and magazine articles on all continents lamented the neglect and abuse of the world's children—and fairly promptly returned to other issues as the summit delegates returned to their own countries.

The fulfilment of all the promises has yet to be seen. Reflecting on the event, Grant observed, 'One had the feeling that the world had finally got its priorities straight, and that a genuine social movement for children had begun to take shape.'[10] But he warned that it would 'take nothing short of precisely such a movement—like the historical movement against slavery, colonialism, apartheid or environmental degradation—to fulfil the promise'.

Green Issues and Greed

Significantly the New York 'world record' for international leadership attendance was to be broken in less than two years by an event that took more politicians and heads of government to Rio de Janeiro, Brazil.

UNCED—the United Nations Conference on Environment and Development—was dedicated to green issues. Agenda items included deforestation and the ozone layer.

Then, as if to underscore matters, there were reports that police and vigilante groups were involved in a citywide 'clean-up' campaign before the event, pushing Rio's street kids off the pavements so that they would not be seen by visiting dignitaries and officials.

According to one reporter, 'Untold numbers of street kids . . . had been simply rounded up and shipped across the Bay to the town of Niteroi. In effect, the Brazilian authorities treated the street kids the way industrialised countries sometimes treat their pollution —by sending them elsewhere.'[11]

In some cases, the young homeless were not just temporarily relocated. They were permanently removed as the city's notorious 'death squads' went into action.

A lone voice of indignation was sounded by British journalist Daniel McGrory, who exposed the sweeps in the *Daily Express*. 'There are many in Britain angry that Brazil lectures us about saving its trees, and does nothing to save its own children,' he wrote.

'We weep at pictures of children dying of hunger, disease and famine, but in Rio they are executed—simply to enable a corrupt and greedy city to protect its luscious reputation.'[12]

The Rights of Children

The focus of so much media attention for that September weekend in New York, albeit briefly, was actually just the latest stop in a slow journey towards a better world for children—one that had begun more than sixty years earlier.

In 1924 the League of Nations, forerunner of the United Nations, passed a ten-point Declaration of the Rights of the Child, which included being granted 'the means needed for . . . normal development, both materially and spiritually'.[13]

Although unenforceable, this early charter 'did provide a guide for countries . . . to consider their children in a new way'.[14] Reports on various aspects of child rights appeared in the following years.

The next major junction on the road to the New York summit came in 1959, when the United Nations General Assembly unanimously adopted the new Declaration of the Rights of the Child. Again without legal force, the document—a revised and updated version of the earlier one—was intended to provide a framework for private and public child welfare actions, based on the assumption that ' "Mankind" owes to the child the best it has to give.'[15]

Twenty years later an effort began to have the Declaration's well-meaning but all-too-often flouted principles backed by the weight of international law. During the International Year of the Child, work started on drafting the Convention on the Rights of the Child. With discussion and examination by governments, non-governmental organisations and international human rights groups—for one week each year—it was to be a decade's task.

Finally in 1989 the Convention was adopted by the UN General Assembly. Its fifty-four articles covered four broad areas of rights:

- survival rights, such as adequate living standards and access to health care

- development rights, including education and recreation, and freedom of religion

- protection rights, covering exploitation and cruelty, and abuses in criminal justice

- participation rights, among them freedom of expression and involvement in decisions affecting their future.[16]

Signatories to the Convention have to file progress reports on their moves to compliance, with a two-yearly update on progress to the UN General Assembly. One of the reasons for the staging of the World Summit was to encourage countries to adopt the Convention, thus requiring them to ensure its standards are reflected in their own laws.

'Like many such documents in history, the Convention is the statement of an ideal which few if any nations have so far achieved,' commented Peter Adamson, editor of UNICEF's annual *State of the World's Children* report, in a background paper to the summit.

It attempts to set minimum standards for child survival, health and education and to provide protection for children who are forced to participate in wars, children who grow up in refugee camps, children who are left to fend for themselves on city streets, children who are exploited at work or in the home, children who are physically or sexually abused, children who are caught up in drug abuse or crime or prostitution.

But as more and more nations ratify its text and begin to enact its provisions into national law, and as the press and public become more concerned to ensure its observance, it may gradually become the standard below which any civilised nation, rich or poor, will be ashamed to fall.[17]

In the twelve months between the Convention's publication and the New York summit, thirty-nine countries signed its agreement. It became the first ever human rights convention to be ratified—a minimum twenty signatories are needed—within a year.

By November 1994, 176 UN member states had signed or ratified, with UNICEF officials saying that they were confident that all of the outstanding countries would have endorsed the Convention by the end of 1995.

While the United Kingdom, Canada, Australia, China, Germany and France were among some of the earlier signatories, the Convention was slow to win approval in the United States—the only Western hemisphere country among the twenty-one members not to have ratified by early 1995.

Opponents warned that 'most of the fifty-four Articles are worded so that many of its provisions could be used against parents in the guise of protecting the child'.[18]

31

Notwithstanding such concerns, the Convention was ratified by more countries more speedily than any other human rights treaty in history.

The Rights of *Street* Children?

While the World Declaration was able to set measurable goals in terms of health and education, in referring to the situation of street children it was noticeably more vague.

Not surprisingly, because no one really knows the extent of the problem. By their very nature, street kids tend to have 'fallen through the net', and so defy accurate quantifying.

The child living under the 'especially difficult circumstances' identified in the Plan of Action will probably not fit into the tidy kind of category suggested by the summit Plan of Action. Likely as not he or she may be 'orphaned or a street child' *because of* being a refugee, or *because of* war or disaster. And as a result any such child is likely to be trapped in exploitation, or slide into juvenile delinquency.

Beyond dispute, though, is that the street children are there. You cannot venture far in most of the big cities of the world without noticing children and youth on the pavements near the subways and bus stations—hanging around aimlessly, guarding a treasured plastic bag of possessions, badgering passers-by for money to buy food.

A World Concern

It is also clear that what has frequently been seen as just a problem of the developing world is now far more common in the West. 'Up to 50,000 young people are homeless in London,' reported the street children's advocacy group Childhope UK in 1991, 'and in other wealthy cities of Europe like Amsterdam, Berlin and Paris . . . it's more common to see young people begging on the streets'.

Youth homelessness is increasing across Europe, with 'every major city in the European Community facing an increasing influx of homeless people, predominantly young and vulnerable'.[19]

For years, the Iron Curtain veiled the reality of unwanted children on the streets of the Eastern Bloc, but the true picture has come grimly into focus since the fall of the Berlin Wall.

More than 200,000 homeless children across Russia were reported by one newspaper, 40,000 in Moscow and 60,000 in St Petersburg.[20]

'We are seeing families today who simply don't care what their children are doing, whether they are begging at subway stations or washing cars,' commented one government aid worker.[21]

According to Graeme Irvine, President of World Vision, there are some 300,000 child prostitutes—under sixteen—in the United States, most of whom have fled homes where they were abused or neglected.[22]

There are differences between the street children of the Two-Thirds World and the West.

The boy in the ragged clothes near the fountains in Rio de Janeiro or on the railway platform in New Delhi is likely to look nine, but he is probably four years older and simply malnourished.

The girl in the skimpy shorts and halter top in New York's Times Square or London's Piccadilly Circus may look seventeen, but she is probably four years younger, and heavily made up.

At the same time, children gravitate to the streets in the developing world at an earlier age—it is not uncommon to find boys and girls as young as five running as part of a gang, their new 'family'. In the West, children generally tend to be older, even young teens, before they are part of the permanent street scene.

But though they may be less obvious in parts of the Western world, where rootless youngsters are still more likely to raise the curious eyebrow of a passing police officer, yet wait a while, or until the city centre crowds have thinned in the late evening, and they will rise to the surface.

Street children or youth are increasingly a world concern. The reasons for their being there may differ in places, but many of their needs remain the same.

Numbering the Needy

If firm statistics are hard to find, that hasn't stopped people trying to set some scale to the problem. Not surprisingly, there are differences of opinion—sometimes more a reflection of the mindset of the estimators than the reality of the situation.

'The number of street children around the world is impossible to calculate with any degree of confidence,' suggested *Newsweek*.[23]

In many countries the government authorities responsible for providing care to such kids cling to outlandishly low estimates, apparently in an effort to deflect criticism at home and abroad.

Relief agencies, which have a vested interest in dramatising the problem, brandish far higher figures . . . Mexico's social services agency declared that there were only 2,278 in the entire country; some private welfare authorities estimate that as many as 1.8 million spend at least half their time living on the streets of Mexico City alone.

One figure commonly quoted by UNICEF and used by many Christian agencies is that of around 100 million street children worldwide. It is a staggering number, and not unexpectedly one that is disputed by some researchers.

One of the factors involved here is the definition of what makes a street child. For those who estimate as many as 100 million, it would include all children and youth who spend a large part of their days and lives on the streets, fending for and feeding themselves.

There may be degrees of hardship and danger, but they would see all of them as needing help.

Those who would offer a more conservative estimate break the street children population down into three categories, the total for which would perhaps reach as many as 100 million, but which would include many not facing situations as desperate as the 'hardliners'.

The first category they identify is *children on the streets*, the largest single group. These children have a home and still 'belong' to a family. They usually go home at night to sleep.

But to help supplement the family's meagre income, they

will spend a large part of their day away from the security and nurture of the home environment, and beyond its protection.

They may find 'honest' but low-paid work, or they may turn to begging and stealing to make money. Their presence on the street puts them at risk from adults who would exploit them, and from the influence of hardcore street gangs.

The second group are usually seen as *children of the street*. They do have some family contact and connection, but it is much looser than the first group. They maintain casual links only, spending far more time on the streets. As such they are more at risk of drifting free from their home, and becoming part of the third group.

These are largely the abandoned, or hardcore *street children* themselves. They may have run away from an abusive home, or been forced out by parents no longer willing or able to care for them; or just been attracted by the lure of freedom from control, with its promise of excitement and adventure.

These kids are on their own, with no one to turn to but the other members of their small group or gang.

Academics who see only this last group as genuine 'street kids' put their number worldwide at around ten million. That may seem small at just a tenth of the other, more broadly-based estimate—but it still makes for an entire population the size of a country like Belgium.

An entire country of children with no proper home, getting by as best they can. There is international concern when a nation is even partly afflicted by famine or disaster; witness the worldwide response to famine in Somalia and carnage in Rwanda.

So perhaps it is about time that world leaders expressed similar concern for this 'hidden country' on the streets of the world's big cities.

Some believe that overplaying the numbers involved actually undermines the intent of seeing something done to help.

Dr Judith Ennew, a long-time street children researcher and advisor, who helped found the now-defunct UK-based Streetwise monitoring group, is among those who suggests a more conservative estimate. But she does not understate the seriousness:

> Those whose only home is the street are among the most unprotected of all children. They have no power and no rights—to care, shelter, education, health. Children without families should be a particular responsibility of the community, but society has usually shown itself unwilling to shoulder that responsibility.[24]

If there is disagreement on precisely how many street children are out there, there is consensus on the fact that the number is growing and, without some concerted attempt to address some of the underlying factors, will continue to grow in the years ahead.

'Unless there is a reversal of current trends, the number of abandoned children is expected to double by the year 2000,' warned World Vision's Irvine.[25]

Leading missionary researcher David Barrett, compiler of the *World Christian Encyclopaedia*, projects the number of 'megacity street children' mushrooming to a staggering 800 million by the year 2200.[26]

He and colleague Todd Johnson base the alarming figure on the anticipated explosion in the number of 'megacities'—with a million-plus population—with the accompanying growth of street kid numbers.

'Global totals are significant only as we look past them to see the big picture—the degree to which Christians are tackling their responsibilities,' observes Barrett.[27]

'The population of the world's cities doubled in the past thirty years and is projected to double again in the next twenty,' warned International Planned Parenthood Federation general secretary and former director general of the World Health Organisation, Halfdan Mahler.[28]

> The human consequences of this phenomenon are frightening to contemplate; we know, for example, that even now over a billion people—a fifth of the world's inhabitants—are either homeless or live in extremely unhealthy conditions.
>
> What commences as a search for improved living conditions [from the rural areas] often ends in squalor and alienation in city slums or begging on the streets of the world's capitals. And it is children, the most vulnerable among the migrants or city dwellers, who suffer most . . .
>
> They have no access to education, basic services or family affection and support. They are an underclass with poor chances for a decent future, condemned to live by deceit, stealing, prostitution or violence. All are 'old' before their time.

Mahler's description applies achingly well to the eighteen-year-old New York prostitute encountered by street worker Trudee Able-Peterson. She asked the teenager what she would most like for her birthday.

'It was one of the saddest things,' said Able-Peterson. 'She wanted a colouring book and crayons . . . When you're robbed of your childhood by these hard-life experiences you're not going to be like other children—and yet your needs are those of any child.'[29]

CHAPTER THREE

FROM CRUSADE TO REVOLUTION

' "Let him alone?" said Noah.
"Why everybody lets him alone enough,
for the matter of that." '

OLIVER TWIST: CHAPTER SIX

Wrong Side of The Tracks

TO THE FIRST-TIME visitor, Howrah Station seems like a riot waiting to happen.

The huge railway terminal in Calcutta—by the banks of the Hooghly, tributary to the sacred River Ganges—is where First World efficiency meets Third World infrastructure in a collision of people.

India has its airports and its highways, but for most people trains—big old steam engines, one of the few enduring and, at least usually, functioning legacies of the years of the British Empire—are the main form of transport.

For travellers and commuters, Howrah is the heart of Calcutta. A city of nine million or more people, and it feels as if half of them are trying to catch a train from Howrah at the same time.

Some race for trains that were late leaving, while others wait for those that never arrived. Families squat together with all their worldly possessions in a few bags around them. Older people appear to be just sitting around until they die, watching the world swirl past.

The noise of countless conversations and arguments fills the high, old colonial-style ceilings of the sprawling station along with the spicy smells of many meals.

In the midst of so much movement—with commuter 'rush hour' times swelling the crowds to crush point—it is easy to miss the youngsters hovering at the edges.

Until you move towards a platform or a food stall, when they will rush forward and hold out begging hands. 'A few rupees for something to eat?'

Scores of young boys make their home at Howṛah, sleeping at the side of platforms and avoiding the police and railway officials on the odd occasion they make a cursory sweep of the area to move people on.

Small gangs jealously guard their platform 'patch' and newcomers have to endure the initiation of a group beating before they are allowed in.

Sumir was just seven years old when he arrived at Howrah, frightened and hungry. 'There were some problems at home,' he recalled. 'I loved my mother very much. One day my father came home and hit her and she died. I was scared, so I ran away and never went back . . . '

A friend took him to Howrah.

The bruises had faded before too long.

During the day he and the others would either beg for money, or go out ragpicking in the neighbourhood, hoping to sell the scraps they gathered for a little money.

A few hours could bring in enough for a meal, and there might even be some to share if another member of the gang was without.

At night the activity around the station would drop to a mere bustle. There would still be people to ask for money from. And then there were the men who would come around and pay the boys to go with them to one of the sheds at the edge of the station.

Sometimes the others would hear screams.

Abandoned Children in Ancient Times

The faded grandeur of Sumir's home for half his life points back a century and a half to the days of the Raj . . . and a period in history which saw the first large-scale emergence of street children.

But if industrialisation and the birth of modern-day cities led to an explosion in the numbers of children left to fend for themselves, abandoned and orphaned children—the runaways and throwaways—have been found from earliest times.

Indeed the Bible's first family included a son sepa-rated from his home by violence. We do not know how old he was, but Cain was probably still a young man when he killed his brother in a fit of temper and jealously.[1] Afterwards he was doomed to be a 'restless wanderer on the earth'.[2]

'Many present-day journalists and people who work with street children assume that this is a relatively new, or recently increasing, phenomenon,' observe Ennew and her former Streetwise co-leader, Brian Milne.[3] 'Far from this being true,

...ncient accounts of street children. Homeless
...cluding children, have always resulted from
...ocial chaos.'

...ically, in Roman times, babies were frequently abandoned in public squares or on the communal rubbish tips—
from where they would be taken in and cared for by others,
often Christian families. The early church father, Tertullian,
observed how 'You [pagans] abandon your children to the
kindness of strangers or to adoption by better parents.'[4]

Parents often 'exposed' their children, as it was termed,
either because they were the wrong sex, or the birth exceeded
the two or three children considered to be the best or 'proper'
family size.

According to noted historian John Boswell, 'Children were
abandoned throughout Europe from Hellenistic antiquity to
the end of the Middle Ages in great numbers, by parents of
every social standing, in a great variety of circumstances.'[5]

He added:

> Parents abandoned their offspring in desperation when they
> were unable to support them, due to poverty or disaster; in
> shame, when they were unwilling to keep them because of
> their physical condition or ancestry—i.e. illegitimate or inces-
> tuous; in self-interest or the interest of another child, when
> inheritance or domestic resources would be compromised by
> another mouth; in hope, when they believed that someone of
> greater means or higher standing might find them and bring
> them up in better circumstances; in resignation, when a child
> was of unwelcome gender or ominous auspices; or in callous-
> ness, if they simply could not be bothered with parenthood.. .

At no point did European society as a whole entertain serious sanctions against the practice. Most ethical systems, in fact, either tolerated or regulated it. Ancient and early Christian moralists sometimes reproached parents for exposing their offspring, but rarely because the act itself was reprehensible; it was usually condemned as a token of irresponsible sexuality, or as a dereliction of some wider duty to state or family.

Almost no ancient writers adduced an inherent obligation of procreator to child; and few writers, in law, narrative or literature, blamed individual parents for exposing children.

That the abandoned and unwanted children were usually rescued from the streets did not necessarily mean that they had been saved from danger, though. 'The children who were rescued were abused in ways that boggle even our jaded minds,' concluded historian C. John Sommerville.

'Children were sold into concubinage by their parents and might live with the children of those who were using them.

'Most Mediterranean cities had boy brothels, sometimes including castrated males used as sexless prostitutes. Abandoned children were raised as gladiators or deliberately maimed to help in begging.'[6]

The Middle Ages

Large numbers of children were also left to fend for themselves on the streets of Europe after the failure of the Children's Crusade, in 1212.

Little is known in great detail about this episode, in which thousands of children responded to what they believed to be a call from God to free Jerusalem from the hands of the Muslims, marching towards the Holy Land from all over Germany and France.

They never made it, with one group apparently being sold into slavery, and the other eventually abandoning their quest and drifting across the countryside in small groups.

'They had so little notion of the world that some of them would ask, as they approached towns on their way to the Mediterranean, "Is that Jerusalem?",' said Pulitzer Prize-winning writer Thomas Powers in his foreword to a new edition of one of the few books to try to investigate what happened.

'A terrible drought afflicted Europe that summer and their route took them through districts which were near famine. Much of the continent was still wilderness, the roads were primitive, and the people were not always friendly,' he noted.

'The sufferings of the children were terrible, and many died along the way.'[7]

The noble if naïve intent of the young crusaders was not enough to protect them from less heavenly-minded adults according to Rev George Zabriskie Gray, the nineteenth-century British clergyman who set out to examine old documents that referred to the event. He reported[8]:

. . . Men and women joined the armies from motives of a baser nature. All that were depraved in every sense found this a rare chance for profit. Abandoned women flocked to them in numbers in the expectation of fulfilling their infamous plans and of robbing as well as ruining the youths. Thieves and sharpers never had such easy prey, and they did not neglect it . . .

Those children who had any money were robbed or cheated of it, and they who had only food in their wallets soon had that stolen by the hangers-on and thieves. The depraved men and women gave way to their passions, so that vice grew daily, and parts of the camp became scenes of sin and lust.

The disorders were increased by the rivalries of subordinate leaders, until at last they moved on, but as little more than a loose, lawless concourse, without chiefs and without discipline. Consequently, they were at the mercy of those who for various reasons saw fit to molest them, and with impunity the wild barons could swoop down upon them from their fastnesses, and seize as many as they would, to hold them in harsh or basest servitude.

But if children and youngsters were at large and at risk in the highways and byways of ancient and medieval times, it is in more modern days that they have become more commonplace and widespread.

From the Industrial Revolution to Today

'The problem is not new in human history . . . ' notes the *Encylopaedia of World Problems and Human Potential.* 'What is new is the scale of the problem. The present-day numbers of street children in single cities like Calcutta may be equal to the total population of those cities'—London and New York, with its nineteenth-century 'ragamuffins' and 'street arabs'—'in the last century.'[9]

The fact is simply a reflection that street children are inextricably linked to centres of large population, where their anonymity secures—or perhaps settles—their 'freedom'.

Caroline Moorhead says:[10]

Street children are born of the failures of development and overwhelming social pressures. They are there as a result of the migration from the countryside into the cities, of poverty, of unemployment, of broken families and the growth of vast urban conglomerations now decaying and bursting under the weight of people. There are no rural street children.

As such, the modern 'generation' of street children were born out of the Industrial Revolution, and the restructuring of Western society from rural, agriculturally based small communities to cities centred on factories and workhouses. In a way, they are paying some of the cost of progress for their parents.

Nowhere was something of the price of social and economic advancement seen more clearly by the mid-1800s than in England, and especially London.

Awareness of the desperate plight of children born into poverty, and of the authorities' inability or unwillingness to help, provoked a Parliamentary reporter. He decided to write an exposé account in fictional form about life for many of London's children.

Charles Dickens' *Oliver Twist* was published in 1838, and immediately won praise for bringing the grim reality of urban street life to people's attention.

Not that everyone was happy to be wiser. Dickens biographer and scholar Norman Page notes that while a young Queen Victoria found the book 'excessively interesting', when she persuaded Lord Melbourne to read it his opinion was:'I don't like those things; I wish to avoid them; I don't like them in reality, and therefore I don't wish them represented.'[11]

The theme of the 'orphan child' was a popular one in literature at the time—abandoned children on the streets of Paris featuring in Victor Hugo's French classic *Les Miserables*, for example.

The novelised commentary on contemporary France's social problems noted how

> . . . it is nothing very uncommon in our present state of civilisation . . . for disrupted households to disperse in darkness, no longer knowing what has become of the children, and leaving them on public highways . . .
>
> It is called, for the sad event has acquired a phrase of its own, 'being thrown on the streets of Paris'. [12]

Yet *Oliver Twist* was the first occasion when the child was presented as the central figure in a major novel. The theme of impoverished childhood was one that Dickens was to return to in many of his later novels.

A century and a half after *Oliver Twist*, the plight of children and young people fending for themselves on the streets of London again became the focus of a literary campaign when Robert Swindell's novel *Stone Cold* won the prestigious 1994 Carnegie Medal for best children's book.

'I feel passionately that we need to tackle the problem of

homelessness,' said the author of his book about a serial killer who preys on homeless teens.[13]

> We're all responsible for each other. And we can't call ourselves a successful society as long as there are people living on the streets . . .
>
> It was the thought that in two, three or four years' time some of the children reading it now could be sleeping rough on the streets of London that made me write it.[14]

While Dickens' classic first brought the orphans and urchins of the cities into the spotlight, it was in another part of the world where the problem of abandoned and homeless youngsters was growing that the term 'street children' was first to be coined.

In his half-yearly report of 1849, George Matsell the chief of New York's police department called attention to the 'deplorable and growing evil' to be found in the city.

He spoke of the 'vagrant, idle and vicious children of both sexes . . . growing up in ignorance and profligacy, only destined to a life of misery, shame and crime, and ultimately a felon's doom'.[15]

> Left, in many instances, to roam day and night wherever their inclination leads them, a large proportion of these juvenile vagrants are in the daily practice of pilfering wherever opportunity offers, and begging where they cannot steal.
>
> In addition to which, the female portion of the youngest class, those who have only seen some eight or twelve summers, are addicted to immoralities of the most loathsome description.

The police chief's report helped prompt the forming of the New York Children's Aid Society, whose founder, Rev Charles Brace, was to refer to the problems and needs of 'the street child' in his later writings.[16]

Announcing the formation of his new organisation, Rev Brace reported how thousands of immigrant boys cast aside by their parents 'sleep on steps, in cellars, in old barns, and in markets . . . '. He went on:

> To sleep in boxes, or under stairways, or in hay-barges on the coldest winter nights, for a mere child, was hard enough; but often to have no food, to be kicked and cuffed by the older ruffians, and shoved about by the police, standing barefooted and in rags under doorways as the winter storm raged, and to know that in all the great city there was not a single door open with a welcome to the little rover—this was harder.[17]

During this same time, back in Dickens' London an Irish student doctor had been appalled to discover a huge underclass of homeless young boys in and around London's East End. Thomas Barnardo encountered ten-year-old Jim Jarvis, and asked the boy if there were many others like him with no home, parents or guardian.

'Oh yes, sir; lots—'eaps on 'em,' replied Jarvis, then taking the medical student to an old marketplace where they climbed the side of an old storage shed.[18]

Barnado recalled later:

> There, on the open roof, lay a confused group of boys, all asleep. I counted eleven. They lay with their heads upon the higher part and their feet in the gutter, in as great a variety of

postures as one may have seen in dogs before a fire—some coiled up, some huddled two or three together, others more apart.

The rags that most of them wore were mere apologies for clothes. One big fellow appeared to be about eighteen, but the ages of the remainder varied, I should say, from nine to fourteen . . . I realised the terrible fact that they were absolutely homeless and destitute, and were almost certainly but samples of many others . . .[19]

Child care movements like those begun by Dr Barnardo, Rev Brace and others—including England's Lord Shaftesbury and his Ragged School Union, which was founded to instruct 'the 30,000 naked, filthy, roaming destitute children of London'[20]—began to work to reduce the numbers on the streets.

But they have continued to exist, with their numbers swollen in times of upheaval and social change. 'In this century, the United States had thousands of vagabond boys and girls during the Depression,' record Ennew and Milne.[21]

Dr Jo Boyden, founder of Children in Development, a project concerned with disadvantaged children, refers to research in 1932 which estimated 'probably half a million juvenile hobos moving around the highways and railroads of the United States'.[22]

Nor was the phenomenon limited to the UK and the USA. Add Ennew and Milne: 'Free youth wandered Germany after the First World War, Italy had its child tramps, and Russia its wild boys.'[23]

But undoubtedly as urbanisation has swollen the world's cities over the past two to three decades, along with inflation and collapsing economies, the numbers of street children have climbed dramatically.

While the numbers of homeless youngsters are growing steadily in the West, they are still dwarfed by those to be found on the streets of the developing world. But before Western eyes look too critically, it is worth remembering that in some ways the Two-Thirds World countries are just playing 'catch up'.

Italian MP Susanna Agnelli, who was a member of a mid-1980s multinational committee set up to investigate the problem of street children to the Independent Commission on International Humanitarian Issues, and who authored the group's report, commented:

> The parallel between street children of the past and the present appears in true light when one reflects that the current transformation of developing countries is a continuation of the process which began in eighteenth-century England.
>
> Its evolving manifestations have reached the remote corners of countries such as Mexico and Bangladesh only now. When it is precisely such Western notions of 'progress' that have aggravated the lot of the marginal child, the West is in no position to preach about the need to cope with their consequences.[24]

The big growth in the world's street children population in recent years is largely due to financial and social poverty. The shoeshine boy on the streets in Manila may have left a cramped shanty home in the slums where there isn't enough money to feed the family. Father drinks to numb the problems, and takes his despair out on mother and children.

The teenage girl begging in Frankfurt may have left a bedroom in her suburban home that was bigger than the Manila family's entire shack. She had her own TV and enough clothes to fill a wardrobe.

But her parents were too busy at work to have much time for her, so when her friends introduced her to soft drugs it seemed like a good kick. Only now it's a habit, not a hobby . . .

While there are differences in the cause and effect of street children's lives between the West and developing countries, there are also, as Agnelli observed,

. . .many features in common.

All those on the street, everywhere, can be described as victims of the crisis of the family. The breakdown of family structure and traditional values, massive emigration, the economic decline of neighbourhoods in the North, and growing sophistication in the cities of the South narrow the difference between streets in different continents.[25]

CHAPTER FOUR

STREETWISE AND STRESSED

'A dirtier and more wretched place
he had never seen.'

OLIVER TWIST: CHAPTER EIGHT

In Hollywood's Shadow

THIS IS MY home,' declared the sign, uneven hand-writing scrawled on a dirty piece of cardboard. It hung over a filthy, torn mattress wedged up in the corner where the slope of the embankment met the underside of the bridge.

The cars that passed overhead, their low rumble filling the semi-darkness, followed one of the main routes that would take them in just a few minutes to the glitzy Hollywood Boulevard.

Lying on the mattress was a girl in her mid-teens, grimy arm half-shielding her bleary eyes from the daylight at the edges of the hidden 'camp' just a stone's throw from some of Los Angeles' brightest lights.

Bags and discarded food wrappings pointed to a sizeable

little community, but only a handful of others were around at midday. Among them some other teens, a couple of older men, heavily tattooed.

And a man probably in his sixties, heavy coat tied closely around him despite the midday heat, sitting away to one side talking to himself.

Beyond The Tourist Brochure

'This is my home,' said **Michael**, pointing to his 'barrow', really just a crude wooden box on wheels.

By day he would trundle it around the streets of Manila's fashionable tourist quarter, Malati, collecting scraps that he would sell to his middleman 'uncle'. At night he would flip the barrow over on its side and curl up inside.

'It is not so good when it gets really cold or wet,' admitted the twelve-year-old. Amenities were close at hand though—a skip across the busy main road and he would be at the water's edge of Manila Bay, where he would wash.

While you do not have to walk too far in most of the world's big cities to stumble across street children, they yet remain something of an unknown—and, as a result, sometimes misunderstood and even misrepresented—population.

Considering their even most conservatively estimated numbers, they are a group more snapshot than documented. In some ways that is not surprising, given that they live on the fringes of society, where they can be conveniently overlooked or ignored.

But as governments and welfare agencies begin to try to address the situation, a number of reports are beginning to emerge that go beyond the sketches and fill in some of the details of street children's lives.

Hidden Hierarchies

One of the most thoroughgoing research projects to date was carried out by Lewis Aptekar, from California's San Jose State University, who spent months systematically documenting and assessing the lives of a group of street children in Cali, one of the largest cities in Colombia.[1]

His research revealed distinct groupings among the children that went unnoticed by the average passer-by.

For example, children below the age of puberty would tend to belong to *camadas*, small groups of two or three linked by friendship, while those who were older were part of *galladas*, larger groups formed around moneymaking—whether through crime or 'small businesses'.

Another distinction to be found as a result of their different ages was different public reactions.

'Much of what happened to them depended on how they were perceived by the public,' he observed. 'Their age, size, and demeanour created an image that contributed to the moral evaluations of the people who saw them. The results of this interplay were vital to the children's lives.

'For example, the younger children were viewed as "cute", but during their physical change into adolescence they came to be perceived as "delinquent".'[2] This value judgement was sharpened when the boys cut off all their hair—a common practice to avoid lice. The shaven-headed young ones were considered even more appealing, while the older ones just looked more thuggish.

Further, Aptekar identified two clear profiles within the younger boys. He separated the true *gamines*—the French word for 'urchin' commonly used of street kids in Colombia—from the *chupagruesos*, which described someone dependent on others.

> The true *gamine* . . . chose to leave home, having rejected the trade-off between childhood protection with family obligations for the freedom from authority with less security.
>
> The second . . . was more a victim of circumstances. Lacking the haughty independence of the *gamines*, *chupagruesos* had not made the clear-cut decision to leave their families and they learned to survive on the streets in a different fashion: by becoming servile to the powerful.[3]

While documenting some of the hardships and hazards they faced on the streets—such as sniffing solvents, violence from adults, concern about finding somewhere safe to sleep—Aptekar yet concluded from his psychological testing and observations that 'most were faring adequately, given their poor circumstances in an impoverished country . . . functioning much better than perceived by the public or press.

'Much of their behaviour is appropriate, productive and psychologically resilient, given their circumstances.'[4]

During the course of his studies, Aptekar also became aware of how readily the street children would change their stories—

about how they came to have left home, how they were coping, what they did to survive—depending on what advantage they thought a certain answer might have.

Indonesia: Pleading Poverty

This chameleon-like, streetwise ability to shape circumstances to their best advantage was reflected, too, in a survey of street children in the Senen market area of central Jakarta.

In addition to collecting and reselling spilled vegetables, collecting recyclable rubbish, cleaning car windows when they stopped at the traffic lights and hiring out umbrellas on rainy days—with half the profits going to the owner—simple begging was a common practice.

Older children without small ones to elicit sympathy—'their plain, cute expressions were enough . . . to move people to give them something'—had to be more aggressive, practically challenging passers-by to give them something.[5]

Sisters **Sugi, Nadewi, Inade** and **Dita** would take it in turns to take along their younger sister Tini, aged three.

[The little girl] looked so deeply saddening—very thin, black, rugged, dirty, full of prickly heat, with dirty, sparse and reddish hair probably caused by frequent sunburn.

Tini had the complete look of a neglected child. She was frequently left naked, or wearing only panties. Sugi or her sister—who was then doing the begging—usually left Tini lying exposed to the sun on the pavement, making her conspicuous enough from a distance, while any of her elder sisters would wait beside her, palms up.

To get people's sympathy, the older sisters frequently made Tini cry by giving her a pinch, pulling her hair, hitting or even dragging her . . .[6]

The same report revealed that more than 60 per cent of those questioned had their first contact with drugs—pills or alcohol common favourites for giving them courage or taking their mind off their problems—within the first year or two of being on the streets.

Paraguay: Shaky Security

One in five street children surveyed in Asuncion, Paraguay[7] worked for nine or more hours a day, making it impossible for many of them to attend school even if they wanted to.

Occupations varied according to age, with begging and car watching commonest amongst the smaller boys as they required little 'training'. As they grew older, though, they were able to 'graduate' to work such as cart pushing at the local market, and street vending—an often dangerous occupation involving darting between cars as they halt at junctions.

Local newspapers frequently reported fatal accidents involving street sellers—among them their own newspaper vendors, a job which, despite the dangers involved, was one of the most highly esteemed around.

When asked why they were working, 64 per cent replied that they needed to work to help the family income, with ten per cent earning money to simply look after themselves. Average daily income was less than one pound—or about a quarter of the country's minimum wage rate.

As the economy suffered, the report noted, street children were caught in a double bind: '. . . like everybody they are affected by the gradual loss of purchasing power of their income. On the other[hand], compensatory economic measures such as price increases and wage increases are only partially transferred to them.'[8]

Contrary to Aptekar's conclusion, the report found that separation from their families created 'an emotional vacuum in the child'. It added: 'He supposedly feels secure, and apparently needs nothing more. It is only when he faces a serious problem . . . that this security—which in fact was just a means of defence—crumbles, and the sensitivity and vulnerability of a hurt or wanting child or youth appears.'

The Philippines: Public Pleas

The child inside the streetwise young person was also revealed in a study of street children in ten cities in the Philippines, outside Latin America the country with among the largest numbers. A third questioned in one city said they wanted to get rich and 'become millionaires', while a third in another wanted to get professional jobs—despite most of them not having finished their schooling.[9]

If the sort of research detailed here has started to give street children a face, there have also been some rare opportunities when they have been given the chance to raise their own voice, as well.

In May of 1990 around a hundred street children from different parts of Metro Manila gathered in the grounds of the

Don Bosco parish centre in the city's Makati district.

The children had been asked to take part in the three-day congress alongside government officials and social workers to talk about their lives and the programmes being offered to help them.

In an open letter to the children of Manila they said:

> We always stop going to school, and some of us have not even gone to school. We transfer from one house to another, and some of us stay in the streets. Some of us live in pushcarts, while others live in old rundown buses. Sometimes our clothes are tattered . . . Sometimes we get our food from the rubbish dump.
>
> Sometimes we beg for food. There are also times we have nothing to eat. We sell, we beg, we steal, we borrow just to make a living. We are beaten up by our parents who are constantly fighting each other. Some of us were abandoned by our parents . . . some were sold . . . we are arrested by policemen for no reason . . . sometimes they beat us and force us to confess violations we did not commit.[10]

Later that same year Brazil saw its second national gathering of street children in Rio de Janeiro, when around 5,000—one of them carried 'crucified' on a giant cross—marched through the city, protesting at the violence they faced.

The USA and Britain: Runaways at Risk

In the Western world, the young people found on the streets

tend to be a few years older than their Third World counter-parts—under-tens are rare—and for the most part runaways.

In 1990, around one million children between the ages of eight and seventeen were living in the streets in the United States, according to youth issues journalist Ellen Switzer.[11]

Patricia Connors, executive director of the Niteline toll-free crisis phone service established by the Covenant House centres for runaways adds:

> Although most of the kids stranded on the street are run-aways—88 per cent, some kids are homeless—11 per cent . . .
>
> Runaways can be younger. but their average age is fifteen or sixteen—47 per cent. Most of them are girls—57 per cent. The majority are white—69 per cent. Black kids—17 per cent, Hispanic kids—8 per cent, and Native American and Asian kids—6 per cent, run away too, but in far fewer numbers'.[12]

In England, the Children's Society has developed a network of 'safe houses' in half a dozen major cities for some of the 100,000 runaways estimated annually across the country.

Most had fled 'intolerable abuse, neglect and rejection', observed director Ian Sparks, with their age—under-sixteens falling outside the means of independent help from govern-ment agencies—leaving them at 'extreme risk'.[13]

A national survey of young runaways in 1994/5 revealed that one in seven had sold sex for money to get by, and more than a quarter had been physically and/or sexually abused while on the streets.[14]

As far as the statistics of the few comprehensive, but localised, studies to date can provide the bare bones of the typical street child, then the collected experiences of those working with and alongside the youngsters can help lay over some of the flesh and features.

From the observations and insights of men and women from four continents it is possible to draw something of a more 'human' profile.

1. The Developing World

They come from families where getting by is such a grind that there isn't much left over for luxuries like time together and affection, even if the parents wanted there to be. It's all about survival.

There may be stepbrothers and stepsisters who are more a rival for food and clothing than family, and a man who isn't father and doesn't particularly want to be. When he drinks the violence spills beyond words into the one-room shack.

The streets are where they are sent to bring back their contribution to the family, and it doesn't matter how many hours that takes. Or where they escape, preferring to face an unknown future to an unpleasant present.

They eat whatever they can.

Their stomachs may not always be empty, but they are probably malnourished. The coppery hair on the Latin-skinned young boy may look charming, but it is a sure sign of serious lack of the right vitamins.

Food is one of the most urgent needs of each day, likely to be bought from one of the local street vendors, or even from a fast food place. Doesn't everyone eat McDonald's?

If there isn't enough money, then there are always the rubbish bins to scour through, the back door of certain restaurants which will toss out the leftovers at the end of the night, and whatever can be snatched from a store.

They sleep where they can feel the safest.

The best bet of all is to have a regular 'home', of which only a handful of others know the location. Maybe a derelict building somewhere, or a covered yard whose walls can be scaled in the dark.

Shop doorways and railway and bus stations offer at least some shelter and a little warmth if there is a blanket to wrap round, but that mostly means catnapping because of the noise and interruptions and dangers.

If this is the case then they may choose to sleep during the day, figuring on greater safety during the daylight hours, especially if they curl up in small groups out in the open near a public place where there are enough people around to offer some security.

The tops of bus shelters can keep them out of reach of the hands or feet of passing adults who might object to their presence, and the grids over subways and cellars offer a blast of warm air on cold days.

If they are fortunate enough to own a pair of shoes they will take them off and slip them under their head so that they will know if someone else tries to snatch them. Any other belongings will be gathered up and clutched in close to their stomach. Spare coins are popped into the mouth.

They earn that money however they can.

Minding people's cars, working as porters, selling things at traffic lights and public squares—food, combs, newspapers, matches, plastic bags—collecting paper and scraps that can be resold, shining shoes.

Begging can be good if there is a sweet-looking youngster alongside and a forlorn expression. Spittle on the hands held out can encourage someone to drop money more hastily, and maybe accidentally more generously.

Sometimes it is possible to slip onto empty trains or buses at the terminus and search the backs of seats for lost coins or pieces of food. Auditoriums and stadiums are worth checking over, too, if a way in can be found.

It is great to be self-employed, but the area might as easily be controlled by a syndicate of adults who demand a certain percentage of what is made.

If steady work cannot be found or is too demanding there are faster, though riskier ways. Snatching handbags from passers-by, reaching out to rip jewellery from around necks, or jackets or wrists. Picking pockets.

And then there is always sex. Straight, homosexual, in motel and hotel rooms, or the back seats of cars, or down dark alleys while a friend watches the main street.

They get sick and stay that way.

Cleanliness may be limited to a dip in the local fountain or river. Even the occasional bath at a shelter or centre will not deal with the body lice.

Pretty soon there is a greasy film on the skin, not to mention the oil and exhaust grease from the roads that coat the feet and lower parts of the leg. It may smell unpleasant to others, but it also means they might slip through someone's grasp if grabbed.

For some the lack of cleanliness and exposure to dirt and grime makes their skin dry, easily cracked.

Teeth go bad. Cuts and bruises are an everyday event, mostly ignored. Infections are commonplace. Even if the injury is serious, chances are the hospital will not want to deal with it.

That leaves the amateur care of friends, or the help of a sympathetic drop-in centre.

Then there are the sexually transmitted diseases they pick up. Even AIDS.

They view other people, adults especially, with a mixture of suspicion and opportunism.

If they are a policeman, security guard or local trader, they are best avoided: if they know your face you are more likely to get blamed for anything that goes wrong in the area.

But if they show an interest in you, then maybe they will part with some money or food. Tourists are a good target because they are still a bit shocked by what they see, unlike many of the local people who try to disregard the youngsters.

They care for just a few others.

The group they become part of is a surrogate, extended family, where there is loyalty and love of a rough-and-ready kind. This is where they get their sense of belonging, and that is a fragile feeling to be defended when necessary.

At the same time it is important to be respected, so a

simple disagreement can become a source of violent conflict. Affection is expressed with kicks, cuffs and punches.

They pass the time in a similarly schizophrenic way.

One moment it might be soccer in the park, or a childish prank along the roadside. Maybe sneaking in to the nearest cinema to see the latest film. Reading—or at least looking at the pictures in—a comic stolen from a newsstand. Listening to a stolen radio.

The next it could be breathing deeply from the neck of a bottle of paint thinner or the top of a can of glue. Nail varnish and paper correction fluid can work, too, if they can be stolen from a counter. Or alcohol.

With a full stomach and a fuzzy head it's time for sex. The leader may have his special girl, but any others are likely to be shared around.

They like the present, but want a different future.

On the streets they are their own person, free to do what they want when they want with no one to tell them no. If there are parents at home, as long as they bring in what is expected of them, not too many questions will likely be asked.

But they don't want to still be here when they are older. They want a home, a partner and a family.

A good job and lots of money—never mind that they haven't finished school, and that their poor diet combined with all the traffic fumes they inhale day after day are likely to cause at least minor brain damage, further limiting their academic capacities and abilities.

Understandably they face not only emotional but psychological stress. 'The life they live reduces their concentration span so far,' remarks Judith Ennew,[15] 'that they find it difficult to sit still and listen.

'The frequent fights in which they are involved are a reflection not just of the violence to which they are subjected on the streets, but also of the "short fuses" they have acquired.'

From her time working with street kids in Bogota, psychologist Anne Balfour observed that they are 'a real paradox; mini-adults one moment, children the next'. And beneath the bravado is deep-seated fear and in-security. She comments, 'They also have a real sense of "aloneness". Not that they are lonely; there are always lots of people around them. But they are often alone; there is part of them that just doesn't give to others. That's because they have to have some kind of strong means to protect themselves from hurt; they have to keep a little shell around them. It can make them seem a bit aloof.'

2. The Developed World

While there are many similarities between Michael in Manila and the young girl under the LA bridge, her options are at the same time considerably reduced.

In the First World, 'traditional values' about children—however insincerely held—actually restrict their choices for getting by, which in some ways only serves to funnel them more directly into desperate dead ends.

Under sixteen the chances of regular paid work are minimal

to non-existent. There are employees prepared to bend the rules and regulations with money-in-the-hand, but not usually when it comes to minors. That is asking for trouble from the authorities.

And then staying out alone on the streets makes them far more conspicuous to either the authorities or would-be abusers than in parts of the world where the culture and climate mean it is not unusual to spend most of the time out of doors.

That rules out sleeping in the open, unless it is hidden enough from sight. Which in turn means having to find a roof, and that means money. Vicious circle.

Which leaves them with only one thing to sell: themselves. Not surprisingly 'a study of runaways aided by the Streetwork Project in New York showed that 86 per cent had been involved in prostitution at some time' said Jo Boyden.[16] 'Estimates suggest that there may be some 8,000 underage prostitutes in Paris, 150,000 in the United States as a whole . . .'

Yet just as people from the same country will share the same national identity while having individual personalities, the world's street children are similar but different.

In the words of Guara Rosa de Silva, who lived on Brazil's streets: 'Let me be a person. Let me live my childhood. Is that too much to ask?'[17]

CHAPTER FIVE

THE KILLING GROUNDS

*'It was the very place for a homeless boy,
who must die in the streets
unless someone helped him.'*

OLIVER TWIST: CHAPTER EIGHT

Brazil

RIO DE JANEIRO enjoys her image as the rich people's playground. The beautiful bodies on Copacabana beach, the European-style pavement cafés.

High above the city, on Corcovado mountain, the statue of Jesus stands with His arms spread wide in welcome. And perhaps also despair.

For Brazil's wealthy seaside city has in recent years also earned a reputation as the poor children's graveyard.

Background noise is almost constant in the Carnival City; traffic, shouts.

So the three vehicles that pulled up near the Candelaria Cathedral sometime after midnight one evening in July 1993 were probably just ignored, if heard at all, by the group of boys sleeping fitfully on the pavement.

Then the men got out. Six of them, carrying guns, according to Roberto dos Santos, director of Rio's Sao Martinho Shelter, well-known among the city's street kids.

'They circled the kids and then opened fire with machine guns,' he said later.[1]

They were assassinated brutally. The killers shot the children in the eyes and in the head.

Seven children died, one survived, but passed away later in hospital.

Two boys were grabbed by the gunmen and taken back to their cars. They were executed and then their bodies dumped nearby at the Museum of Modern Art.

'They came out firing,' recalled a survivor from the group.[2] 'One was shooting at me, but his gun misfired. I ducked, then ran and ran . . . '

Although the murder of street kids in Brazil has been well documented for several years now, this largescale killing—ironically, at the site of a large candlelit vigil to highlight the violence street kids face daily, just a few months earlier—shocked even a nation numbed by routine death.

Itamar Franco, the country's President, himself flew to Rio, saying he felt the murders 'like a punch in the face', and launching a high-level investigation into the massacre.

It came as little surprise to many that the three men arrested soon afterwards in connection with the attack turned out to be military policemen.

For many of those who form the feared 'death squads' that

roam many of Brazil's cities are said by the street kids and their few advocates to be officers—either earning some extra off-duty money through violent 'freelancing', or simply taking the law into their own hands.

Such was the case in the Cathedral killings, with reports of a quarrel sometime before the shootings, between some of the homeless youngsters who congregate in the area and a group of policemen.

'You'll regret this. We're gonna get you,' one of the officers had called out, according to one report.[3]

If the ferocity and brazenness of the attack horrified the average Brazilian—and people around the world—it did little to surprise those who look out for the interests of the street kids.

Amnesty International began documenting 'death squad murders' several years ago. Their research even led to a blunt newspaper campaign in Britain in 1990, relating some of their findings: 'Brazil has solved the problem of how to keep kids off the street. Kill them.'

Typical of the cases they have on file is that of Patricio Hilario da Silva, aged nine. His spindly corpse was found dumped in an open space in the fashionable Rio suburb of Ipanema in May 1989.

A note tied around his neck read: 'I killed you because you didn't study and had no future . . . The government must not allow the streets of the city to be invaded by kids.'

An Amnesty International report later that same year said that at least one child each day was victim to the death squads, and warned that as more youngsters were forced onto the streets to look for work to help to support desperate families, growing numbers were at risk.

As reports of the murder of street children grew from the mid-1980s onwards, the Brazilian government finally responded to concern—much of it expressed by other countries—by enacting legislation intended to protect the country's many abandoned and homeless youngsters, and founding a Ministry of the Child.

It established a National Commission to Combat Violence Against Children and Adolescents, which reported:

> According to Federal Police sources, there were 4,611 executions of children and adolescents in the years 1988, 1989 and 1990, giving an annual average of approximately 1,533.
>
> These figures . . . have been the only objective figures obtained at the national level to be published to disseminate the problem in Brazil and abroad.[4]

Many suspect that the official figures are much too low. In an earlier report by the Centre for the Mobilisation of Marginalised Populations,[5] a human rights group, researcher Leontina Soares noted how it was not always possible to determine the cause of death.

In a survey of deaths registered in three township police stations in Rio State, besides explicit cases of murder were included 'natural death cases, cases in which children were run over by cars, death by hanging, fatal casualties, etc., in which it was impossible to establish whether death had resulted from a genuine accident or from the intention of a third party—that is, deliberate homicide'.

Brazilian journalist Gilberto Dimenstein decided to look for himself behind the occasional headlines that documented the latest death, travelling the country to talk with the street kids, their helpers and protectors, and even some of the killers.

To his horror he found widespread cases. Street kids almost everywhere knew of someone, maybe even a friend, who had been killed.

The occasional flurry of national and international media coverage of the killings had led to changes. But simply in the way that the killers operate.

'To keep their actions out of the news, they bury their victims in secret cemeteries and threaten their families with trouble if they talk,' he reported.[6]

Since 1989, when the killing of street children began to receive publicity in the national and international press, Rio de Janeiro's more experienced crime reporters have noticed how much more rare it has become to see the bodies of young death-squad victims lying in the street or in ditches at the roadside . . .

Reporters remember one occasion when a murdered child lay in a street of Greater Rio for more than a month.

According to one human rights watchdog group, the city's police department 'admitted that half the city's unidentified death squads are policemen. Nonetheless, Brazilian authorities have failed to take action to stop these death squads and punish those responsible for such abuses'.[7]

Perversely the killings have led to children unwanted while they were alive being adopted after their death. For bodies which arrive at the Legal Medical Institute bearing marks of violence need a death certificate bearing a name before they can be buried.

If no one claims the body, it cannot be buried. 'The social welfare organisations have found an imaginative way out of this dilemma,' explained Dimenstein.[8] 'They find parents willing to adopt the child posthumously, and give it their family name.'

'It is a sad irony,' Maria Tereza Moura, a former co-ordinator of Rio's Street Children Movement, told him. 'A macabre game. A boy who spent his life on his own gets a father only after he's dead.'[9]

While killings were so frequent that they usually warranted no more than a paragraph or two in one of the local newspapers—and people would casually step round bodies left in the street[10]—one particularly brutal attack did make major news in 1991.

A group of armed men burst into a shed in a *favela*—or slum area—where seven street children aged between nine and seventeen were gathered to sniff glue and share the spoils of their day's thieving.[11]

The men, who said they were police, accused them of having stolen a pair of tennis shoes, tied the children up at gunpoint and dragged them to a nearby stream. There they beat them, forced them to lie down, and shot each of them in the back of the neck.

Amazingly, one of them—a sixteen-year-old girl—survived when the bullet somehow deflected off her bone and lodged in her skin. She held her breath and pretended to be dead.

She told a national magazine later: 'They aimed at them one by one. I was the third, and the last was the youngest, Claudio. The four men argued over who would shoot the boy, everyone wanted to kill him.'[12]

Guatemala

While the work of the 'death squads' in Brazil is perhaps most widespread and undoubtedly best known internationally, that is by no means the only country to kill its street children.

Amnesty International files also document many cases from Guatemala, where in the capital alone an estimated 5,000 children live rough on the streets.

In June 1991 six teenage boys were bundled into a station wagon from the streets of Guatemala City by a group of armed men and driven away.[13] The bodies of two of them were identified the following month. They had been shot in the head. Their ears and tongues had been cut out, and their eyes burned or gouged out—traditional marks left on the body of an informer.

In another case earlier that year, thirteen-year-old Nahaman Lopez was set upon by men while standing on a street corner with his friends. The others managed to run away, but he was caught and badly beaten. He died in hospital ten days later 'of multiple injuries, including a ruptured liver, six fractured ribs, two broken fingers and severe bruising to 70 per cent of his body'.[14] According to one report, just before he died the young boy whispered to the social worker at his hospital bedside: 'All I wanted to be was a kid. But they wouldn't let me.'

Colombia

In Bogota, Colombia, posters went up around the city inviting people to attend the forthcoming funerals of the 'delinquents of the zone' who were to be 'exterminated', according to journalist Tim Ross.[15]

'After machine-gunning three young drug dealers . . . the professional gunmen . . . scattered leaflets saying that this was just a warning of what was to come and signing themselves "Vigilantes of the Night",' he wrote.[16]

Twelve-year-old Marcos Fidel Quisquinay was approached by a man who handed him a bag and asked him to take it to a fast food restaurant elsewhere in the capital.

As he arrived there a bomb planted inside the bag exploded, killing him and injuring seven other people. 'There was nothing left of him. His body was strewn about everywhere,' said an eyewitness.[17]

Those responsible are not always so public about their actions. Many times the bodies lie undiscovered or hidden.

Gruesome confirmation that accurate statistics for the number of killings in places like Colombia are difficult, if not impossible, to come by presented itself when 'a landslide uncovered several murdered children'.[18]

Death may not come as calculatingly in other parts of the world, but it still finds children on the streets where violence is an everyday fact of life.

Martin Graham, who works with the Future Hope rescue programme for boys in Calcutta recalls a time when 'a child who had stolen something, a young boy, was caught and severely beaten around the head with staves. By the time Tim'—one of the other members of staff—'got to him he was dead. He was about eight years old.'

The Philippines

Ray was on the streets of Manila for several years after being abandoned on a bus by his parents and being unable to find his way home again. He joined a gang, began pickpocketing and stealing what he could.

He and the others had several run-ins with different junior police officers in the area, who would punch and kick them. Then one night he and a couple of friends were picked up by some men and taken away to some open land in another part of the city.

'One of the men had a rifle and pointed it at me and told me to go. I ran as fast as I could. They shot but missed, and I just kept running and hid. I thought when I saw them that they were killers.'

Irish priest Father Shay Cullen, who has worked with street children in Olongapo City, north of Manila, for a quarter of a century, said that during his time in the country 'many children have been murdered on the streets of our city'.

Speaking at the House of Commons, London, he said: 'One of my staff, a former street boy, who now works with the children, is the lone survivor of a gang of twelve children.

'The rest of them were summarily executed in the back alleys of Olongapo because they were an annoyance to tourists and they disturbed the smooth operation of the nightclub life.'[19]

'You've Got to Kill Them'

From Colombia, street children's advocates have reported cases of youngsters being killed because it was feared that they were carrying the AIDS virus.[20]

Countries like Brazil seem able to live with the violent death of their children because for most of the population the scruffy kids they pass on the street are nameless nuisances, to be feared if not ignored.

After the Cathedral massacre in Rio, many people called in to a local radio station to applaud the killings.[21] 'Everyone is making them out to be heroes, but they were not sweet flowers,' a local taxi driver told journalists.

Dimenstein found a similar disregard. A shop owner who helped pay for one of the death squads operating on the outskirts of Sao Paolo explained:

Nobody wants the kids to get killed. The problem is that there is no other solution. If they get arrested, the courts just let them go and they are free to steal again. And my shop continues to be under threat. Don't I have the right to run my shop in peace?[22]

A former member of a death squad told how they operated:

What happens is that you are employed by a group of shopkeepers. You earn more than a policeman. A boy comes along and robs the shop, so you give him a thump. Another one comes along and steals something else. If you don't do anything and let them go on stealing, you lose your job.

It's no use playing about with some of these kids, you've got to kill them.[23]

Above: *Sleeping during the day hopefully means safety at night on Philippine streets.* © *World Vision: Bongo Go.*

Left: *Five year old Rosie behind bars in Olongapo city. Rescued by Fr. Shay Cullen who works in partnership with Jubilee to protect children of the Philippines.* © *Preda Foundation/Jubilee.*

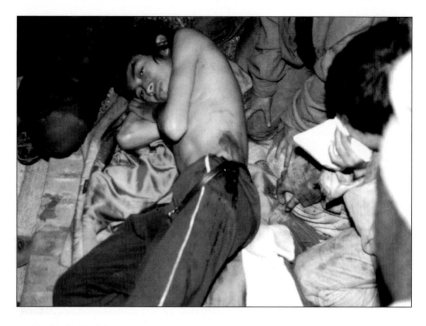

Above: *Violence is common. This boy had been stabbed in the back with scissors.*

Left: *This youngster has lived on the streets for seven of his twelve years.*

Above: *A street children family—their home is a handcart—Brazil.*

Below: *A boy receiving free hot food supplied by local street kids ministry—Brazil.*

Above: *An abandoned child's body found on a beach in Rio.* Newsweek *magazine estimates that three children a day are murdered by death squads.*
© O. Povo/Jubilee

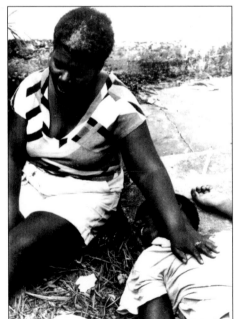

Left: *A mother weeps for her murdered child.*
© O. Povo/Jubilee

Above: *Caged children awaiting their fate.*

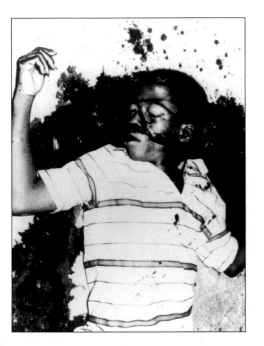

Left: *A murdered boy in Brazil.*

Above: *Street boy whose 'home' is at the side of the platform of Howrah Station, Calcutta, India.*
Below: *Violence is never far away in the lives of street children. It could even be over a thrown-away piece of bread..*

Above: *Birds have nests, but the Nairobi street children have no roof over their head. The city pavement is good a bed as any.*

Below: *We have to stick together. Yes, birds of a feather stick together.*

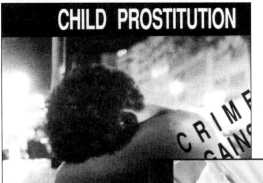

Left:
Postcard to The United Nations organised by the Jubilee Campaign highlighting the sexual exploitation of children worldwide.

Right:
Postcard to The Presidente de la Republica of Guatemala organised by Jubilee Campaign high-lighting the murder and ill treatment of street children by the Guatemalan Police.

STOP KILLING STREET CHILDREN!

Below: *John Major with Roberto dos Santos, director of Sao Martinho shelter in Brazil and Jubilee's Aninha Capaldi who has volunteered her time as director of appeals. The Prime Minister raised the issue of the continued murder of street children at the Earth Summit in June 1992.*

Nor are such views always just held privately. As Caroline Moorhead reported:

> In one large Latin American city the officially licensed radio station . . . broadcast a suggestion that citizens should take matters into their own hands and put an end to the children who are infesting their streets. The result, for a while, was that an average of two street children were found dead every day.[24]

No Favours for The Famous

If the street children's facelessness and namelessness makes them targets for unquestioned, easily accepted killing, then it might be expected that some sort of public recognition might offer a form of security. Not so.

Fernando da Silva Ramos was a typical Brazilian street kid who became internationally recognised in the early 1980s, after starring in Hector Babenco's acclaimed film *Pixote*.

The gritty true-to-life film about a group of street kids and their tangles with the law, drugs and prison—played by eleven-year-old Ramos and a group of other real-life street children—was one of the first times the issue was addressed in the mass media.

It made a star of Ramos, at least for a brief time. He appeared in a couple of other films, and even a commercial for UNICEF. Soon, though, he was back on the streets again, and on 27 August, 1987 he was killed by police in Sao Paolo. According to Dimenstein, 'Banners saying, "Pixote was a crook. The people are grateful to the police" appeared in the streets.'[25]

Giovani Garcia blushed and forgot his carefully prepared words to the First Lady of Guatemala when his time came to hand over a bouquet of flowers at the official opening of the Childhope organisation's offices in the country, in 1987.

The President's wife covered the awkwardness of the four-teen-year-old former street kid by reaching forward to give him a hug and a kiss. The cameras clicked.

Still looking only twelve, the boy known as 'Penguin' in the years he had spent on the streets, continued to do well adjust-ing to a new life for the next few years, until something tugged him back when he was eighteen.

His body was found dumped outside Guatemala City. He had been shot in the head at point-blank range. His hands were burned beyond recognition and there were signs of other torture.

The Childhope worker who had befriended Giovani said later:'Sometimes I think he almost made it. Other times I know that he did make it. They just moved the finish line a lot closer.'[26]

The Earth Summit that took so many world leaders to Rio led British Prime Minister John Major to Roberto de Santos' shelter. There he met some of the young boys who visited the centre, among them **Juanito Jose da Silva**.

The tall teenager had run away from home when he was only six, drifting into crime and glue sniffing on the Rio streets. He seemed to be going nowhere until he arrived at the centre one day.

Through contact with the staff, he started to change, help-ing with the younger children, renewing contact with his family, and working hard at different jobs. His dream was to become a chef.

He was proud to be chosen to perform a traditional dance as a welcome to the British premier, an event captured by the world's television cameras.

Three months later he was killed by gunfire in one of the city's many *favelas*.

Everyday Violence

If in some places the assassination squads are a way of death, then even more is violence a way of life for street children around the world. It is as much a part of their every day as eating and sleeping.

Often it is meted out at the hands of shopkeepers or local residents, or vigilante groups hired to harass and intimidate. Frequently, too, it comes from policemen and security guards.

Among cases documented by street children workers in Guatemala City were those in which:

- two fourteen-year-olds and a twelve-year-old were accosted by police who forced them to swallow the glue they were sniffing.

- Juan Carlos, aged fourteen, was snatched and taken to the basement of a police training centre where dogs were set on him.

- Jose Vasquez, aged sixteen, was abducted and taken to parkland where, hooded, he was stripped naked, tied to a tree, beaten and burned with cigarettes.[27]

A common form of 'punishment' by police in Brazil is to bind boys over a bar with their hands behind their backs, so they are suspended upside down by the knees, and then beat them with truncheons.

Seventeen-year-old Jose told of another favourite trick of patrolmen. 'We like to jump up and ride on the back of buses, so they wait until the buses are moving, then pull up alongside and hit us hard with their rubber sticks to try to make us fall off.'

Nor is the violence limited to outsiders. Fights often break out between boys on the street. It could be between members of rival gangs, or even between friends over a perceived slight.

Rogerio pulled up his T-shirt to reveal a huge tract of twisted purplish flesh across his side, where the scorched skin has scarred and twisted.

He had gone with another boy's girl, and when the other discovered he had been cheated on, he crept up while Rogerio was sleeping.

The rival took the bottle of 'thinners' from which he sniffed to get high, splashed it over his sleeping victim and dropped a lighted match.

In a former garage converted into a hostel and day centre for street kids in Manila, social worker Nic Arriola pulled a bag out of a drawer in his office and showed some of the arsenal he had confiscated. From boys as young as eight.

The brutal-looking weapons showed considerable home-made ingenuity. There were several knives made from broken glass, string or tape bound around one end to make a safe handle. A slingshot, sharpened nails with wooden 'handles' bound onto them, a car aerial that could be whipped down hard.

'We don't let them in if they are carrying something,' said Nic as he fingered a couple of forks with the handles bent backwards in a circle and two of the teeth pushed out forward so that they could be gripped firmly like a knuckle duster.

'They are frightened of killing somebody, but once they have they really have a name in the gang,' said Johan Lukasse, at the halfway house he and his wife, Jeannette, founded in Belo Horizonte, Brazil.

'It could be an enemy, a member of another gang, or a policeman, or whoever. When they have, they are really somebody. And that is important to them—often it is the reason they have run away from home, because they feel like a nobody there.

'So if you can cut it on the streets, if you make a gang leader, that really gives you a name, an identity. If you are fast or strong, you get recognised for that, too. Once they have it, they don't want to lose that—because it is all they have.'

And then there is perhaps the ultimate violence.

Iain Brown left home at thirteen, spending much of the next three years on the streets of San Francisco and Hollywood, selling himself and getting heavier into drugs.[28]

Eventually he went home to try and make a new start. Things seemed to be working out. Then, shortly after a family Christmas, Iain hanged himself from a tree at the back of his parents' home.

He was nineteen.

CHAPTER SIX

BODIES FOR SALE

'It will make you cry, I believe,
to hear what he can tell . . .'

OLIVER TWIST: CHAPTER FIFTY-ONE

Manila

JULIE IS eighteen years old, looks thirty, and says that most days she feels sixty.

She has lived on the streets since running away from home at the age of eight, and usually sleeps in the hallway of an old, rundown building in Manila's Ermita district, under the stairs.

As the evening arrives, she tidies herself up as best she can, smoothes out some of the wrinkles from her dirty, crumpled grey dress and goes off to sell sex.

She aims for two customers a night, just enough to tide her over to the next day. She charges about two pounds, but will settle for a third of that at a pinch.

'I don't really like doing it,' she admits expressionlessly, lank hair, lifeless eyes. 'But it's better to get paid for it than to have to go on doing it with my stepfather for free.'

Julie is one of an estimated 8,000 children and teenagers who stock the 'shelves' of Manila's infamous red light district.

To the casual stroller, the streets of discos and girlie bars adjoining the Philippine capital's exclusive tourist districts actually seem quite tame.

There are the neon lights, the gaudy signs and the smiling girls outside the doors who flash a sample of their bodies as you pass, but it all seems rather restrained, really.

Certainly not as blatant as the sex streets of other cities. Like Amsterdam, where some of the live clubs screen hardcore movies in their foyers, and the shops display all that's on offer without leaving anything to the imagination.

But, then, razor blades seem harmless enough until you unwrap them, and behind Ermita's little more than saucy facade is a sex industry as ugly as you will find anywhere. Under-age is the speciality.

Inside many of the clubs, young girls in bikinis dance on top of the bars and tables to tinny music, with smiles welded to their face as the visitors leer up at them. They earn a couple of pounds a night this way, but the big money comes when they go back to the hotels.

Others, like Julie, simply hang around outside, or cruise some of the area's restaurants and cafes. Everyone knows why they are there.

Some are run by pimps, like **Jocelyn**. Now thirteen, she started selling sweets on the streets three years earlier. Dad was dying from cancer and mum just couldn't make ends meet.[1]

Then came the day an elderly, smart-looking lady asked her if she'd like to earn some 'big, easy money'. Of course.

Next thing she knew she was in a small hotel room where a foreigner, an old man, was undressing her . . .

Now she is out three to four nights a week, hoping to find a Japanese tourist, because they pay best. When the clients are arranged through her pimp, Rollo, he gets a cut but she doesn't mind because he keeps her supplied with solvent 'to ensure a good performance . . . she feels extra daring and uninhibited—at least for the next four hours'.[2]

If the Southeast Asia region is the shopping centre of the world for paedophiles, then Manila is one of its most fashionable stores. Nor is it just girls. Many of the youngsters who prostitute themselves are boys.

Like **Richard**, who drifted away from home when his mother took up with another man. 'There were stepsisters and stepbrothers; they didn't like me. I don't think my mother really cared about me, either.'

He found his way to the city, sleeping in a park for two nights without anything to eat before being befriended by a man. He fed him, and took him home. Like many other young boys and teenagers selling themselves to older men, he finds it hard to admit. 'I . . . would go with guys and bad men,' he says vaguely.

Sometimes the children sell their bodies not only with their parents' knowledge or acquiescence, but their actual help. Ten-year-old Totoy's father encouraged him to 'befriend' a middle-aged German tourist, who then gave money to the family.[3]

In another instance 'the parents of a thirteen-year-old girl took her to her abuser's hotel room, waited, and left with their daughter' and the money.[4]

89

Sex Tourism

The 'tourist sex' industry thrives throughout the region. A third of the estimated three million prostitutes in Thailand are said to be children.

Sri Lanka has around 10,000 eight- to fourteen-year-olds servicing visiting holidaymakers, the majority of them boys, unlike most other places.

Research that revealed a 'dramatic increase' in recent years in the number of child prostitutes in Sri Lanka, the Philippines, Thailand and Taiwan, led in 1990 to the founding of an international campaign, ECPAT—End Child Prostitution in Asian Tourism.

According to international coordinator Ron O'Grady, there is 'a large international network of paedophiles who are visiting and often living permanently in Southeast Asia'.[5]

And in a cruel deception 'some have opened what they described as "orphanages" or "street shelters" for poor children. These apparently compassionate deeds are actually fronts for paedophile organisations who use them as centres to provide young people to visiting paedophiles'.

Fear as well as perversity has fuelled the demand for younger partners. Researchers have noted that concern about contracting AIDS has heightened the desirability of fresh flesh—turning buyers to 'ten- to twelve-year-olds, but even children as young as eight'.[6]

The rising demand for young virgins has led brothel keepers to a twisted scheme for keeping the customers happy. Reveals O'Grady: 'With modern technology, hymens can be restitched and plastic containers of blood inserted in a girl's vagina enabling her to be sold as a virgin several times over and still be able to furnish proof of her virginity.'[7]

Subic Bay

Sex tourism is 'the ultimate in exploitation' in the opinion of Father Cullen. His outspoken views and actions have not always made him popular in the bayside city of Olongapo; he has faced deportation three times, and death threats.

But he continues to offer a home and hope for the future to needy street children—and to campaign for known abusers to be brought to justice.

The city, in Subic Bay, virtually ran on prostitution during the years it was home to a United States naval base to which ships from the Seventh Fleet would return regularly for periods of 'R & R'. But some of that 'rest and relaxation' was of a chilling nature.

A report by Britain's Jubilee Campaign revealed some shocking incidents, among them the case of an eighteen-month-old child found to have gonorrhea; her mother was living with three US sailors at the time.[8]

In addition, they disclosed that an undercover investigation by US Navy officials discovered that children as young as four were being sold for sex with US seamen. Yet while eight suspects were identified as pimps, none were arrested or brought to trial.

Perhaps the most horrific case documented, though, concerned twelve-year-old Rosario Baluyot. She died in hospital in 1989 from blood poisoning after an emergency operation failed to save her. Doctors had removed a broken vibrator from inside her vagina.[9]

It had been inserted by a 36-year-old Austrian medical graduate who took the young girl and a fourteen-year-old street boy back to his hotel room after selecting them from a group of youngsters at the side of the road.

The man was subsequently found guilty of rape and homicide, and sentenced to life imprisonment. He was released after two years, on a technicality.

Subic Bay Naval Base finally closed late in 1992. The departing sailors left behind them not only many scarred and broken young bodies, but also around 5,000 Amerasian children, of mixed parentage.

At the time of writing, Father Cullen was attempting to pursue a lawsuit filed in the United States against the US Navy and the authorities of Olongapo City for the 'systematic abuse of children . . . by sailors'.

America and Europe

Prostitution and pornography are almost certain destinations for young teens—of both sexes—who leave homes in North America and Europe.

Eric ended up in Los Angeles after a chain of events— family fights, petty crime, trying to start again, being passed between separated parents, and abused—that left him without money and no idea of how to get any.

An older man, clean and friendly, got talking to him as Eric dawdled over a coffee in a cafe. Asked how long he had been in town and what he planned to do. When Eric admitted he didn't know, the man offered—just as a favour, a short-term measure, you understand—that he could sleep on the floor. 'No funny stuff.'

It went that way for two nights. Then, on the third, he felt the guy crawl under the covers with him. Caught between shock and gratitude, he didn't move.

Broad and blond, Eric stayed. He got introduced to drugs that took away some of those awkward feelings. Then the man suggested a good-paying job. Modelling. For gay magazines—wrestling, that kind of thing.

After a while, the man brought another youngster home. It was time for Eric to move on. He found himself back out on the streets with his bagful of belongings. But this time a bit more wise and a little less particular. He found that it was easy to make 150 pounds a night with the right man. Not that the money went so far, with the drugs and all . . .

Workers at the Covenant House shelters in New York and California reckon that most of the young people who arrive looking for help have been involved in some form of sex-for-sale. And they despair at the laws that in some parts mean it is illegal for a sixteen-year-old to drink, drive or vote—but they can appear in a pornographic film.

Seventy per cent of the teenagers who arrived at the Children's Society's 'safe house' in Manchester, England, had been involved in some form of sexual exploitation, according to one survey.

For many young runaways, sex and drugs become a vicious downward cycle. They need the drugs to dampen the shame, and they need to expose themselves to those feelings to earn the money for the drugs.

Whereas street kids in the developing world mostly stay with solvents and perhaps marijuana, in the West it is far more common to move onto harder drugs: cocaine, heroin, even the deadly 'crack'.

Olga Hernandez, medical sister at Covenant House, told TV documentary maker Peter Lee Wright the youngsters they saw with HIV-related illnesses were mostly drug addicts: 'Not IV drug abusers, though, crack addicts. What we see is kids who go into crack houses and come out three days later, and all they did was exchange sex for crack. There's no money exchanged, there is nothing else but they have sex. They don't know whether they have sex with three men or 300, both males and females.'[10]

Young girls taken under the wing of 'friends'—who quickly turn into pimps—will introduce them to drugs and then use their addiction as a control to keep them working. It can be a fast slide from the fancy hotel rooms and the big money to the back seat of cars and wasteland for a fraction of their former price.

When their sex currency gets low enough, young girls can find themselves serving other purposes. The whores become 'mules'—smuggling drugs in swallowed condoms, because their youth usually puts them beyond suspicion.

Michelle and Liz, both in their early teens, made the run from London to New York until one of the contraceptives burst inside Michelle's stomach and the cocaine spilled out, killing her.[11]

Disease

In addition to the emotional scars and the physical violence, the youngsters selling their bodies also face the danger of sexually transmitted diseases—with deadly syphilis returning after being almost nonexistent for many years, and gonorrhoea increasing.

Then there is AIDS. With street children a mobile, largely overlooked population, there is no real way of knowing just how far the virus may have spread already. But many fear that it is a time bomb, ticking away on the pavements.

Drug use and prostitution are not the only reasons they are at risk. It is not uncommon for street boys to sleep with each other, with gang rape used as a punishment for some misdemeanour. And if a street girl loses her 'man', she is immediately up for grabs.

Strangely, though, the dark cloud that is the unknown quantity of the AIDS problem may in some way have a silver lining. For 'the issue of street children is being brought to the forefront of the public agenda by the issue of AIDS. Until now we have dealt badly with street children and ignored them,' delegates to an international AIDS conference were told in 1990.[12]

The number of cases of AIDS in Belo Horizonte has already reached a level where one of the groups working with street children has bought a home exclusively to house those dying from the virus.

The Lukasses and their co-workers take in the mothers—little more than children themselves—and the babies that are being born to them, with the virus. 'Because they are already malnourished and in ill health from living on the streets, they are less resistant once the virus develops,' said Jeannette Lukasse.

Typically, despite its headline-making nature, AIDS is a distant concern for the youngsters themselves. As Reina, a prostitute for almost half her fifteen years on the streets, reasoned: 'Why should I worry about dying from AIDS in a year, when I could be dead tonight?'[13]

But if the street children themselves are not worried about AIDS, its presence in their community can be just another factor pushing them beyond other people's desire to reach out and help them.

As the Lukasses were preparing to open their AIDS home, local newspapers told the story of a street boy dying from AIDS who was driven round in an ambulance for four days, with each hospital refusing him admission.[14]

'He died on the fourth day, right there in the ambulance...'

Slave Labour

While growing concern about AIDS highlights how children are exploited sexually on the streets, it is not the only way that their bodies are being used for others' gain.

Millions find themselves caught in different levels of slave labour, working long hours in poor and often dangerous conditions for minimal wages.

Founder of the international street children's advocacy group Childhope, Peter Tacon, observes that while in many countries labour and child welfare regulations prohibit children from working under the age of twelve or fourteen, such codes do not 'accommodate the cold facts of poverty or the basic human needs of food, shelter and clothing'.[15]

With this in mind, his concern is 'not laws to prevent children from all work, but ways to prevent abuse and exploitation of children in their places of work . . . Since unjust economic circumstances have already demanded that children work or perish, the very least we can offer is the guarantee that our youngest workers will not be further wounded.'[16]

There are physical dangers for the children—often the younger ones, because they are thought to be harder to resist buying from—selling matches, flowers, cigarettes and sweets among the traffic queues of Lima.

They risk cuts and infection as they scavenge among rubbish skips for plastic bottles that can be resold, old newspapers that can be recycled—work that has to be started early, around 5 a.m., to be sure of the best pickings.

They also face violence and extortion often from adults who control them. Like Joned, who controlled operations in part of the Senen Shopping Centre in Jakarta so tightly that it was known as 'the danger zone' by shoeshine boys.[17]

He demanded a cut of any money made by boys working in the area, and any 'unauthorised' youngsters he came across, he would confiscate their shoeshining kit and forcibly take all their money from them.

Police and security guards will often use their size and strength to take money, confiscate goods, beat and rape, if they are not 'appeased'.

In some parts the exploitation even takes place in the name of God. Newspapers in Senegal, West Africa, have railed against the 'disguised child slavery' they say results in hundreds of children begging from tourists in city streets.[18]

Asking for *Sarax ngir Yalla*—'charity for God'—is endemic, 'rooted in the religious practice of the majority' who as Muslims are taught that 'those with enough to eat are obliged to give to those without. Those who have nothing to eat have the right to demand of others.'[19]

In many other parts of the world, too, religious views of life perpetuate, if not create, situations of extreme hardship.

While crushing economic problems are behind India's millions of homeless, the Hindu belief in reincarnation and karma—that someone's lot in this life is the reward or cost of how they were in a previous existence—causes many not to want to interfere in the gods' dealings by offering a helping hand.

The country is said to have the largest population of working children in the world—estimates range anywhere between 15 million and 49 million—though many of them are not 'street children' in the big cities, but from rural families, based in factories and workshops out in the rural areas.

Yet many children are also to be found working in cities like Calcutta, where young boys serve as general dogsbodies in cramped motor shops and repair yards—close to dangerous fumes and equipment.

One informal survey estimated that 67 per cent of the children worked between eleven and fifteen hours a day, with a further 20 per cent working sixteen to eighteen hours.

A study by the Institute of Psychological and Educational Research in the city found that as well as often working in dangerous and unhealthy surroundings—with sicknesses like bronchial asthma, tonsillitis and eye complaints common—many of the working children were also educationally and emotionally deprived as a result.[20]

'The birth of many an adult criminal can be traced to the group of teenage child workers who develop a thwarted personality due to the lack of proper socialisation,' it concluded.

Desperation can encourage dangerous ingenuity, especially in a city—described by one American visitor as 'a necropolis: a city of the dead and dying'—where the streets are lined with more people than there are alms to go round: countless whole families whose home is the pavement, hands held out for any passing help.

Some of the boys from Howrah station saw a new potential source of income when they looked out across the Hooghly at the ghats on the far side—the stepped temple and shrine sites along the side of the river where Hindus would ceremonially wash and pray.

'We would wait until the people had left and then dive for the coins they had thrown in. You could collect good money in two or three hours,' said fourteen-year-old Milthu. But it meant a risky plunge into the murky water of the strongly flowing river, especially avoiding the ferries and boats that passed frequently.

'Some boys drowned. I was doing it one day and a strong wake from one of the boats washed over me; someone caught me and pulled me out.'

International 'child trafficking' is not only for prostitution or illegal adoptions, but also for cheap workers, according to investigative journalist Tim Tate.[21]

He cited Defence of Children International records for Yugoslavia, 1986 which noted that:

> Many street children in Italy have been virtually sold into slavery by their parents in impoverished regions...
>
> Once smuggled into Italy, they are forcibly tutored by their gypsy captors in the ways of a life of petty crime. The slave traffic from Yugoslavia has existed for years . . . Some officials in Rome estimate that more than 10,000 Yugoslav children have been imported to Italy and held in gypsy encampments outside major cities. . .

Following the illicit trade in children-for-sale led Duncan and Jenni Dyason to a shocking discovery in Guatemala City, where they worked with a street children project.

They began to investigate after being offered money for their own baby daughter one day, and were later followed by a couple who tried to snatch her from their arms.

A trainee lawyer 'told them she knew of a hospital . . . where children were taken for the removal of eyes and other organs'.[22] When asked for more information, the woman 'pulled her finger across her throat, saying she valued her life, and asked them to leave'.[23]

CHAPTER SEVEN

THE MISSING MISSION

'. . . the expense . . .
and all for a naughty orphan
nobody can love . . .'

OLIVER TWIST: CHAPTER THREE

The Second 'Summit'

GLEN EYRIE IS an English castle in a Hollywood sort of way. The early-1900s edifice stands in the lee of the Garden of the Gods, a picturesque rockland area at Colorado Springs, at the foot of one of the Rocky Mountains' most famous peaks.

Built by American Civil War veteran General William Jackson Palmer as his retirement home, the Tudor-style building has for the past forty years been the headquarters of the Navigators, committed to Bible-based discipleship and service.

And in 1992, it was the setting for a Christian counterpoint to the New York summit of world leaders. Executive officers and other senior figures from over forty major missionary organisations and agencies gathered for the annual conference of the Evangelical Foreign Missions Association. The theme: reaching the world's children.

Explaining the choice of the 'small half' theme for a conference more usually considering topics like management, fundraising and church planting strategies, EFMA executive director Paul McKaughan said simply: 'To talk about reaching the unreached, and to ignore children and young people, is to base our strategy on a false foundation.'[1]

Amid the welter of statistics, it fell to Doug Nichols to champion the case of street children. Now based in the United States, after several years working among street kids in the Philippines, he oversees the work of ACTION International, one of the few mission agencies currently focusing on the needs of street kids.

Quoting the estimate of 100 million street children around the world, he asked the assembled leaders:

Does this estimate bother you? Would it if your child, or grandchild, was among them?

If you counted one child per second, that would be sixty per minute, or 3,600 in one hour. At the same rate in twenty-four hours, without sleep, you would reach 86,400. It would take over twenty-three days to count two million. All 100 million street children of the world would take over three years and two months to count. And every unit counted is not a mere figure; it represents a living child, loved by God and purchased by Christ's blood. One hundred million. Think of it!

Some of these children are young and cute. They can still smile. But most are older, have rotten teeth, and are scar-faced, disease-ridden, flea-and-lice-infested, shifty-eyed, suspicious, and fearful. They are the poor, the outcast, the abandoned, the exploited . . . the children of the streets.[2]

Nichols went on to throw down a challenge to those mission leaders present to radically rethink many of their existing strategies and activities to invest more effort in reaching out to street kids.

While his plea won wide acclaim at the conference, in concrete terms it remains to date something of a cry in the wilderness. There have been one or two encouraging echoes, though.

Southern Baptist Foreign Mission Board associate director for Research and Planning, John Cheyne, proposed street children as a 'new frontier' in missions in an article for his denomination.

With the majority of street children growing up in totally non-Christian environments, most 'know nothing of Christ as Saviour', he observed.[3]

> If they consider the church at all, it is in terms of its failure to care . . .
>
> Where are the churches? Generally, not in the slums. Not on the street corners. Not targeting the 145 million children around the world who represent one of the largest homogenous groups of unreached and lost within their own countries.
>
> Isn't it past time we considered seriously this new 'frontier' as a target for evangelism and for just plain caring?
>
> Tomorrow may be too late.

World Horizons, based in the UK, promoted Brazil's street kids as an 'unreached people group' in a magazine profile appealing for support for their work in the South American country.

They reported the story of the six-year-old son of a wealthy

Argentinian family who became separated from them at Buenos Aires airport, somehow slipping unnoticed into a Brazil-bound plane.

At the other end he again passed unchecked through official channels, getting lost in downtown Belo Horizonte. 'There he spent his first night, cold, hungry, lonely and very frightened. He cried himself to sleep under one of the bridges, calling out to a Mum and Dad who never came . . . '

After six years of hand-to-mouth survival by begging, scavenging and stealing, he told his story to a visiting journalist writing about street kids. Initially sceptical, the writer investigated, found the disappearance was true, and effected a happy reunion.

'A happy ending indeed,' said World Horizons, 'but for seven million others in Brazil there is no happy ending—just the desperate, daily struggle to survive. Each night, their cries—like those of the young boy—go unheeded by anyone. Yet their cries are heard by God.'

Two years after the Glen Eyrie gathering, the words spoken there seemed to have fallen on many deaf ears.

'Missions' Blind Spots'

Attending another major missions conference, Compassion International President Wesley Stafford decided to track how many times 'children' were spoken of—and heard the word 'only a dozen times . . . and never in a strategic sense to reach them apart from their parents'.[4]

While some of the agencies represented at Glen Eyrie are

beginning to wrestle with some of the issues involved in what means—for many—a far-ranging reappraisal of much activity, much of the missions world has yet to seriously embrace Nichols' call.

To do so means facing the blunt reality stated by World Vision Vice-President Bryant Myers, that children and youth are a 'significant blind spot in Christian mission'.[5]

'If children and youth are as central to the mission task as I believe, then our way of thinking about mission and contextualising the gospel today will be seen to be inadequate.'

Correcting the error will involve rethinking some common values, shattering some myths, and facing some hard questions.

One of the unspoken values of much missionary activity is a perhaps unconscious reflection of life in the home church—a living example of the Bible truth that we reproduce after our own kind. Birds give birth to birds. Dogs give birth to dogs. And churches that treat children as second-class citizens here will give birth to mission works that treat children as second-class citizens there.

This is not wilful neglect so much as damage by default—which stems from the view that while 'children's work' is OK in a nice little corner, the real church is all about adults.

It should not be too surprising that children living on the margins of societies either overseas or at the other end of town do not compel our attention if the youngsters in our own church or community are viewed at best as an inconvenience and at worst as simply in the way.

This 'adults only' attitude to the Kingdom of God—which

runs contrary to Jesus' warning that we should become like little children if we want to see it—is a reflection of the way many churches have turned salvation from a matter of faith to a question of intellect.

If becoming a Christian is about knowing the right things—rather than the right person—then it becomes reserved for those whom we believe can really grasp the finer points of our preaching. This is the gospel for grown-ups. Children and the feeble-minded need not apply . . .

The consequences of this mind-set can be seen in churches where the children are shepherded out into inadequate rooms at the back of the sanctuary while their parents get to stay behind and stretch out in newly-bought chairs to hear the sermon; where a few determined mothers and the 'graduates' of the youth group teach class week in and week out, while the men get on with the really serious spiritual work of stewarding and serving communion for the adults; and where the monthly 'family worship' bores the adults and patronises the youngsters.

All of this underlines how often we see the children as the church of tomorrow—when they grow up and are responsible enough to sit still without doodling in the hymn books.

If for these reasons and others we can, even unknowingly, pay lip service to the well-dressed children that we know, how much easier to simply ignore the dirty-clothed ones we don't.

Part of the reason for this attitude could also be unconsciously, sincerely practical; the average adult convert is actually going to be more 'useful' in the long run. They can share their testimony, join the outreach committee, and give their money, all of which will help the church be more effective in its work and mission.

And after all, the Bible does tell us to be good stewards. Just consider it a matter of wise investment.

The Great Commission

This mix of principle and pragmatism is at the heart of much mission activity in the last years of the twentieth century, as the approach of the close of the second millennium has spurred scores of agencies and denominations to set their goals contributing towards the completion of the Great Commission: the taking of the gospel to every people group in the world.

Their embracing Jesus' 'final command' centres on the paradox that as Christians we may all be the same, but we are still different.

On the one hand, the apostle Paul writing to the Galatians makes it clear that any allegiances or associations before coming to Christ are now secondary. 'There is neither Jew nor Greek, slave nor free, male nor female, for you are all one in Christ Jesus,' he emphasises.[6]

Yet implicit in Jesus' Great Commission is the recognition of wide differences between people. For His command to 'go into all the world' enjoins the disciples to preach the gospel to 'all nations'. But the word in the original Greek is *ethne*, meaning 'a people' rather than a country as shown on a map.

According to missiologists, a people group is distinct from others by virtue of factors of language, lifestyle, location. An 'unreached' people group will not hear the gospel without someone from outside their group going and becoming a part of their world.

As a result, many current mission initiatives advocate specialised, focused ministries that concentrate on a particular group, and ways of presenting the gospel that may connect with that 'people' but no other.

Similar thinking is behind the 'church growth' movement on the home missions front, where churches tailor services to individual interest groups, be they singles over-thirty, or divorcees, or heavy metal music fans.

To be practical, any attempt to take on a specific people group has to have something that will attract and sustain the interest and involvement of a wide group of Christians; both those prepared to go, and those willing and able to support from the rear, whether that be through finances or prayer or both.

Poor Prospects . . .

In such 'public relations' terms, street children as a group fall a long way behind most of the other unreached people groups whose colourful culture and noble history can inspire and enthral. In crude 'marketing' terms, street children don't have a lot going for them.

The Berbers of the sub-Sahara with their camels, flowing blue robes, striking features and slave-trading history of centuries, may offer an altogether more satisfying appeal than Ricardo and his glue-sniffing followers, grimy-faced and graceless as they sift through the rubbish bins of Bogota.

The everyday street kid is not particularly photogenic. Life on the pavements produces a ruggedness and roughness that challenges the creativity of the average photographer to turn the typical street corner tough into the dirty-faced angel favoured for fundraising advertisements.

Ministry to street children is also unusually high investment, low return.

Although a group, they commonly have to be reached individually, one at a time. By nature they may be mistrustful and untrustworthy; building a solid relationship with just one can take weeks and months, and then there is the chance they might throw it all over and go back to their old ways.

'Some missions despair of working with street children,' recognised urban missions expert Dr Timothy Monsma, 'because the prospects of rapid church growth appear rather dim for this type of evangelistic effort.'[7]

Impacting a whole city or neighbourhood population of street children, then, needs many people who are ready and willing to put in many hours, feeding, clothing, caring.

Materials and manpower cost money, and in an age where 'decisions' are sometimes included in the annual report like a business's fiscal account, there may not be a lot to show at the end of the year.

Street children are also missed by many current missions and evangelism methods. A large number cannot read, so literature distribution does not work. They are not a target audience for rallies and special meetings. Most of them also slip through the net of child sponsorship programmes.

Street kids are 'continually by-passed' by most current approaches of this kind, maintains Nichols.

Counting the Cost

If all this means that ministry to street children is a hard one for which to win committed supporters, it is also a difficult one for which to recruit the workers prepared for the often thankless long-haul.

In countries 'closed' to traditional missionary endeavours, Christians can still gain access to the people by going as 'tent-makers'—taking their regular skills as doctors or teachers, and seeking to share their faith as the opportunities arise.

With street children there is no similar subtle—if not without its risks—approach. Taking the gospel to them means doing so on their terms, and on their turf.

It means being out and about in dangerous parts of the city at the wrong time of day and night. It means being sure to shower well on getting home to wash away any lice that may have been picked up through contact with the youngsters, and carrying surgical gloves to be ready to tend to any wounds without risk of infection.

Ron Homenuke is a broad-shouldered Canadian, a former ice hockey player well capable of looking after himself, yet he admits to being anxious at times when he is on the streets of Manila among teenagers half his size and weight.

'The drug scene is downright scary,' he says. 'Very regularly the newspapers give reports about some drugged lunatic or pot-head that has killed someone.'[8] Despite hygiene precautions, he has caught chickenpox, typhoid and hepatitis from contact with his young street friends.

Among a volatile population often experienced in crime beyond their years, there is also the ever-present threat of violence. Youthful moods fuelled by drugs can mean a young friend one moment can be a deadly enemy the next.

Even after years of experience have taught him to read situations quickly and know how to diffuse trouble, Johan Lukasse has been the target of blows and bricks, and more than one death threat.

And then there can be danger from unexpected quarters. British-born Bruce Harris walks the streets of Guatemala City in a bullet-proof jacket because of the warnings he has received.

As director of the Casa Alianza project—which includes a night shelter and rehabilitation home—he has catalogued the violence suffered by street children at the hands of police and private 'security' workers, and pressed for prosecution of the offenders.

His campaign for justice has not been universally popular. One night in July 1991, four men in an unmarked car pulled up outside the crisis centre and screamed: 'We are going to gun down Bruce Harris and then kill the staff and the children, too.' As they drove off—'We thought it was just another threat', Harris said, 'until the car reappeared and sprayed the front of the building with machine-gun fire.'

Samoan Mati Galli ended up in hospital in Belo Horizonte after being snatched from the streets by off-duty policemen, beaten and tortured.

Whether they mistook him for one of the gang, or were just annoyed that he was showing an interest in them remains unclear, but he was beaten and dragged away to a waiting car late one night.

During the next few hours the Youth With A Mission worker was driven to different police stations around the city, beaten and punched. The men who abducted him strung a noose around his neck, jammed one gun into his mouth and another against the side of his head.

While he recovered from his injuries, leaders John and Jeannette Lukasse lodged an official complaint with the city authorities.

In a rare example of justice, a year later three policemen were found guilty of assaulting Galli, and detained. However, one of those sentenced to two years was seen back on duty after just twelve months.

As the verdicts were announced, Johan Lukasse said that he hoped that the court case might mean street kids could sleep easier on Belo's pavements. 'We cannot guarantee that, because a lot of these kind of incidents go on without witnesses being around,' he observed. 'However, we do believe that those involved . . . will be more careful in the future, which can only be good for the children.'

Johan's wife was able to measure things for herself some months after the case when she awoke in the middle of the night to noises in the halfway house below her family's quarters. Going to investigate she found six armed policemen searching the premises after a break-in at another building, attributed to some of the boys at the hostel.

The officers grabbed one of the teenagers and started to manhandle him roughly to their car, ignoring Jeannette's requests to be allowed to go with them. But when they passed the 'YWAM' sign outside the building, they eased up.

'They said, "Oh we didn't know you were YWAM." They took off with him, and we feared that they would really beat him up. But they brought him back in just half an hour, which was a miracle. I believe that his quick release had something to do with the association the name YWAM has for policemen; some of them still remember the case,' she said.

'But overall, kids do still get tortured and beaten. They still get killed by hired murderers.'

Fear has kept some would-be helpers from the streets, according to former Danish social worker Flemming Kjaer, who directs the work of Pan de Vida—'Bread of Life', in Spanish—an umbrella group for Christian organisations working with street children in Colombia.

Potential volunteers have thought twice because of the many murders linked to the country's cartels.

'There are very few Westerners working with street children in the country,' he said. 'In some cases it's fear putting people off. There have been many cases of young Christians who wanted to come and help, who have not been allowed to by their parents because of their concern for what might happen.'

He knows the dangers personally—he and his family once received an anonymous bomb threat at their home—and 'understands the feelings'. But he believes that 'sometimes the Western church has forgotten that as Christians we are already sacrificed to God's purposes. That can mean the risk of losing one's life . . .'

But if because of faulty thinking or fear the Church of the late twentieth century has not really taken on the street children of the world as a mission field in their own right, there is still hope.

For doing so—hearing the charge of the likes of McKaughan, Myers, and Nichols—will not necessitate a new revelation so much as the reawakening of a rich missionary heritage.

CHAPTER EIGHT

THE 'CHILDREN OR CHINA' CHOICE

*'Thank heaven upon your knees . . . that
you had friends to care for and
keep you in your childhood.'*

OLIVER TWIST: CHAPTER FORTY

The Passage House

JOSANNA SAT ON the pavement on the edge of the Passage to Hell. That is the name they give to the Independence Square area in Recife, Brazil. Where the girls could hustle a little money by selling their bodies to the tourists and cruisers—and their souls into the bargain. 'It's the fastest way to get to hell,' they would joke without laughing.

An eleven-year-old runaway from a broken home, raped when she was younger, Josanna nursed the bruises from a fresh beating by a passing policeman who had objected to her speaking out of turn.

As Ana Vasconcelos sat down beside the girl, who was drawing in the dirt, she saw that the picture taking shape in the dust was a house.[1] But no ordinary home. This one was all crooked, distorted, out of shape.

115

'Why is it broken?' Ana asked.

'Because that's how I am,' came the reply.

A moment's silence as the former lawyer and the girl sat together and contemplated the sketch in front of them. Then a question to the woman.

'Why can't we be born twice?'

Ana was surprised, confused, she recalled later. 'What do you mean?' she asked.

'I don't like this life. I would like to have another one . . .'

Josanna told how she had even tried to kill herself to start over again, only failed in the attempt. The people at the hospital had patched her up and told her not to be silly, that you couldn't be born again.

It would be hard to find a more profound picture of the desperate search of street children around the world than in this moving first encounter Ana was to have with a homeless young girl, or one that speaks more powerfully to the Christian heart.

The successful lawyer's response has been to throw her considerable talents and energies into the founding of The Passage House—a home and haven in which girls can be helped to reroute their lives, turning their backs on the Passage to Hell and instead, says Ana, 'building a passageway to heaven'.

While for Ana the heaven she has in mind is more manmade than God-governed—where street girls can come to terms with and take charge of their lives through their own determination and some professional help—there have been others to whom it is a literal place and a laudable goal.

George Müller

Almost a century after his death in England, the name of German-born George Müller is still synonymous with dynamic faith, trusting God for the impossible. By the time he died, aged ninety-three, he had seen over $1.4 million given to his ministry, all of it without direct fundraising or requests for money. What is sometimes overlooked in the faith lessons of the man is that most of the money he received was given to support his caring of some of the many homeless and orphaned children in Bristol—the 'poor, neglected children' he saw 'running about the streets'.[2]

The man who originally felt himself called to be a missionary 'among the heathen' instead found himself caring for abandoned youngsters—by 1869 his then world-famous orphanages were home to no less than 2,000. 'The Lord, for I cannot but think it was He, again and again brought the thought of poor children to my mind,' he remembered.[3]

Müller's work was shaped by his admiration for the orphan houses founded in the late 1690s in his homeland by Professor August Francke—'the largest enterprise for poor children then existing in the world'.[4] He stayed in lodgings in one of the homes in Halle for a short time during his early days as a preacher, and later emulated much of what he saw.

But if his method was borrowed from Francke, his missionary heart in his care for the children came from the Bible. In 1837 he recorded how Psalm 68:6's reference to God as 'father to the fatherless' had been 'a special blessing to me, with reference to the orphans'. He wrote in his journal:

The truth, which is contained in this, I never realised so much as today. By the help of God, this shall be my argument before Him, respecting the orphans, in the hour of need.

He is their father, and therefore has pledged Himself, as it were, to provide for them and care for them; and I have only to remind Him of the need of these poor children, in order to have it supplied. My soul is still more enlarged respecting orphans. This word, 'a father to the fatherless', contains enough encouragement to cast thousands of orphans upon the loving heart of God.[5]

Barnardo's

Nor was Müller alone in switching the focus of his missionary vision from far-off lands to the nearby streets. When Thomas Barnardo arrived in London from Ireland in 1866, it was with the intention of studying as a doctor so that he might go to China to serve as a medical missionary.

But 'almost as soon as he set foot in London he began to draw out from their dark holes-and-corners a race of wild, unloved, and outcast children, a race which skulked and suffered there for generations while the life of the city went on around them'.[6]

The young medical student first worked with William Booth's fledgling Salvation Army in the early months of its pioneering work in some of the roughest parts of London. From there he went to help out with an evening school for young boys through which one of the students—young Jim Jarvis—introduced him to the hidden world of the capital's street children.

Caring for the homeless youngsters he came across, as best he could, and speaking about their needs whenever possible, yet Barnardo continued to prepare for China until one day a letter arrived offering him a thousand pounds—if he would give up the idea of going overseas, and stay in England to help the destitute children.

The man who was to lead to the founding of Dr Barnardo's Homes around the world had found his mission field closer to home. 'I did not choose this path,' he later reflected.[7] 'My Father called me . . . I may say, without any presumption, that the work among destitute children which I have been permitted to carry on has, from the first, afforded a remarkable example of the reality of God's guiding hand in the affairs of life.'

Later in life he reflected: 'We were enabled to renounce a life of usefulness in another and more distant land.'[8] And: 'Of the divine character of our mission we have no doubt.'[9]

His conviction that the needs of the homeless, abandoned children of London were as much a matter of missionary endeavour as the millions of Chinese who had not heard the gospel was shared by William Booth.

On learning of the young doctor's change of plan, Booth responded: 'You look after the children and I'll look after the adults. Then together we'll convert the world.'[10]

The New York Children's Aid Society

As immigration and urbanisation went hand in hand to

'import' street children to the New World, so a similar response was found there.

Charles Loring Brace became aware of New York's growing numbers of street children when he went to work as a city missioner in the Five Points area around 1850. In 1853 he was asked by a group of leading men in New York to head what they called 'a mission to the children': the New York Children's Aid Society.

In the organisation's first public circular, Brace argued that: 'As Christian men, we cannot look upon this great multitude of unhappy, deserted, and degraded boys and girls without feeling our responsibility to God for them.'[11]

We remember that they have the same capacities, the same need of kind and good influences, and the same immortality, as the little ones in our own homes. We bear in mind that One died for them, even as for the children of the rich and the happy . . .

For the most part, the boys grow up utterly by themselves. No one cares for them and they care for no one. Some live by begging, by petty pilferings, by bold robbery . . . The girls, too often, grow up even more pitiable and deserted . . . They grow up passionate, ungoverned; with no love or kindness ever to soften the heart. We all know their short, wild life, and the sad end.[12]

In the years that followed, the NYCAS was to support almost fifty projects in New York, including industrial schools, lodging houses and a summer home. The organisation was to be best known, however, for developing a programme of 'placing out' whereby tens of thousands of abandoned children were gathered from the city and sent to the rural West, where they were placed with families in return for helping work the land.

Applauded in its day, the programme has been criticised in more recent times for inappropriately removing children from their home environment, where there might have been, albeit inadequate, contact with their parents and siblings.

However, assessing the system from the late 1990s is difficult, observes historian Marilyn Holt, who concedes that 'when faced with what urban life offered the poor—street life, crime, prostitution, overwhelming deprivations, incarcerations, and little hope for escape—the argument must swing to Brace's heartfelt appeals for relocation'.[13]

Father Don Bosco

The Protestant Church was not alone in trying to meet the needs of the rising numbers of homeless children. In Turin, Italy, Catholic priest Don Bosco began a work 'rescuing waifs, founding "boys' towns"'[14] after an orphaned beggar boy crept into his church one morning to shelter from the cold.

He opened schools, workshops and youth centres, eventually winning respect and renown for his initially misunderstood and unappreciated work. Despite the acclaim, he insisted: 'I am only Don Bosco, friend of street kids.'

Founding the Salesian brotherhood in 1859, he dedicated his life to taking in young boys, giving them general and religious education. 'You can do nothing with children unless you win their confidence and love,' he reasoned, 'by bringing them into touch with oneself, by breaking through all the hindrances that keep them at a distance.'[15]

Father Bosco's order continues its caring for boys around the world today, in places like Manila and Calcutta—where the brothers at a small home in the centre of the city work among the street boys living in and around the slum district made famous by Dominic Lapierre's book *City of Joy*.

Modern-day Models

Back in England, others were following the lead of Barnardo and Booth. Civil servant Edward Rudolf, the superintendent of teachers in a Sunday school in Lambeth, 'was disturbed by the daily spectacle of tens of thousands of destitute children on the streets of central London'.[16]

'His own childhood had been poverty-stricken—but nothing like that. So in 1881 he founded the Waifs and Strays Society'—later to change its name to the **Church of England Children's Society**, as which it continues to work with homeless children and teenagers today.

The particular risks of the young girls left to fend for themselves on the city streets were to move another city missioner to do something almost half a century later. Christian Missionary Alliance worker Emma Whittemore was alarmed at the plight of the 'street girls—young girls who, in most instances, had been taken advantage of because of poverty or family problems'.[17] Her first **Door of Hope** missions centre opened in 1890, and by 1931 there were almost 100 similar centres across the United States and Canada, and in Africa, China and Japan.

More recently, the founding of two of today's largest Christian agencies for the care of children in need in developing parts of the world—World Vision and Compassion—were prompted by exposure to the needs of some of the many abandoned children found on the streets of Korea after the 1950s war there.

Evangelist and filmmaker Bob Pierce—whose maxim was: 'Let my heart be broken by the things that break the heart of God'—was moved by the poverty and hunger he encountered in his travels through China and Korea.

Founding **World Vision** in 1950, he became an advocate for children, recognising the urgent need to care for the hundreds orphaned by the Korean War.

Visiting that country in 1952, American evangelist Everett Swanson was heartbroken by what he saw:

> Trucks made daily rounds in the mornings, picking up children who had frozen to death on the streets during the night. Children who survived were desperate.
>
> Orphans had become a burden to society. There were no local infrastructures that were willing to reach out to them. The church was almost non-existent . . .[18]

Swanson's concern led him to raise money for Christian children's homes, and the establishing of **Compassion International**.

Today World Vision and Compassion are multi-million dollar organisations, involved in child sponsorship, education, relief and development programmes in scores of countries.

While the likes of Barnardo, Brace and Müller stand out in the history books because of the scale of their efforts in response to the growing need around them, practical care for abandoned children did not only begin following the Industrial Revolution.

Diana Garland, dean of social work at the Southern Baptist Theological Seminary in Kentucky and organiser of the Southern Baptist Child Advocacy Network notes that the early church 'was well known in Roman society for rescuing infants and children who would otherwise perish'.[19]

Child abandonment continued in Europe and America until the eighteenth century. In addition, many children were orphaned by wars and epidemics. In response, Christians continued to seek out and care for these children. They took children into their own homes and often adopted them. When the needs became too great, churches built institutions—orphanages and children's homes.[20]

CHAPTER NINE

'DON'T LOSE THE LITTLE ONES'

'Find him, find him out, that's all!'

OLIVER TWIST: CHAPTER THREE

The Third 'Summit'

WHILE THE GATHERINGS of heads of state and missionary leaders, in New York and at Colorado Springs, highlighted the plight of many of the world's children and the Church's failure to respond adequately, her duty to do so was established in less official surroundings, among a group of friends in Capernaum, on the shores of Israel's Sea of Galilee.

Jesus' twelve apprentices had seen Him model great humility in the preceding months. He had healed the sick, dazzled crowds with His wisdom, yet been content to share what He had and stay where He could without demanding special treatment.

They missed it.

Perhaps they were jockeying for position, when they came to Jesus and asked: 'Who is the greatest in the kingdom of heaven?'[1] Their order of merit seems to have been a deeply rooted concern, for even after Jesus had put them straight twice about godly greatness, two of them would yet later try to secure special seating in heaven.[2]

Jesus' main concern was to impress upon His disciples the topsy-turvy nature of spiritual as opposed to worldly greatness. But He also saw the opportunity to instil another value that overturned those of the day.

Most likely He was teaching in the open air, with children milling around on the edges of the group. They may have been ignored by their elders, but Jesus noticed them. He called one over.

It is worth remembering that Jesus said or did nothing by accident, only what He was given by the Father.[3] This was not just a casual incident, a chance occurrence. For the One who could move on, leaving behind people not healed and questions unanswered, to be sure of completing all He had to accomplish in a short time, this was a deliberate part of what He wanted to leave with His disciples.

'I tell you the truth,' He said, 'unless you change and become like little children, you will never enter the kingdom of heaven.'[4] Furthermore, He warned that 'Whoever welcomes a little child like this in my name welcomes me. But if anyone causes one of these little ones . . . to sin, it would be better for him to have a large millstone hung around his neck and to be drowned in the depths of the sea.'[5]

In a culture where children were 'seen and not heard', relegated to the back of the synagogue with their mothers, the idea that they could be used to teach men anything would have been revolutionary enough. Sommerville notes that 'in making the child the model of the life of faith, he exactly reversed the expectations of His listeners'.[6]

He gauges Jesus' elevation of the youngster as 'the most positive assessment of the child's worth up to that point, and perhaps in all history'.[7]

Lest anyone be tempted to dismiss His gathering close of the child as simply a visual aid for an object lesson in humility, Jesus added: 'See that you do not look down on one of these little ones.'[8]

Jesus' Concern for Children

Implicit in His closing remark was God's viewing of adults and children as equals. For in telling the disciples that 'their angels in heaven always see the face of my Father in heaven'[9]— the text from which people draw the idea of guardian angels— He was underlining that they were of as much concern to God as the grown-ups who took comfort in the promise of Psalm 91 that the Lord would 'command his angels concerning you, to guard you in all your ways'.[10]

Here in this passage, too, is found Jesus' 'missionary heart' for children—in His story of the Lost Sheep. Most commonly this parable is preached from the longer version in Luke[11]— like all good teachers, Jesus was likely to use the same basic outline more than once—which focuses on repentant 'sinners', usually taken to be adults.

But told in Capernaum, the story revealed something more, about Jesus' concern for lost children in particular. For here, when He spoke of the man who left the ninety-nine to go in search of the one who had wandered away, it was in the context of His talking of 'the little ones'. And He concluded that: 'In the same way, your Father in heaven is not willing that any of these little ones should be lost.'[12]

Another parable illustrated Jesus' desire to see all people—whether young, poor or sick—brought into His kingdom. In the story of the Great Banquet, the servants are sent out 'into the streets' to 'bring in the poor, the crippled, the blind and the lame', when the first-invited guests decline the invitation with a series of self-centred excuses.[13]

While Bible scholars agree that Jesus was probably using the child He called to His arms to illustrate the need for His disciples to hold a right attitude of heart to all, including 'young believers', it seems clear that Jesus did not want the significance of what He was saying about children to be lost, either. For He returned to the topic to underscore it within a short time.

The disciples cannot have fully understood what Jesus was telling them in Capernaum, because a little later they tried to stop a group of children from seeing Jesus. He obviously had more important things to do than bother with children, they reasoned.

They could not have been more wrong. For all His patient, slow nurturing of His friends in the ways of the kingdom of heaven, this time, as they dismissed the children as of no consequence and an intrusion on what really mattered, He grew 'indignant'.[14]

But Jesus told them: 'Let the little children come to me, and do not hinder them, for the kingdom of God belongs to such as these.'[15] And he 'took the children in his arms, put his hands on them and blessed them'.[16]

Jesus and the Needy

As well as overturning attitudes to children, Jesus also consistently challenged His followers that His kingdom was for the needy and downcast. He chose to begin His public ministry by reading in the synagogue at Nazareth from the book of Isaiah.

' "The Spirit of the Lord is on me, because he has anointed me to preach good news to the poor . . . ",' he read, adding, 'Today this scripture is fulfilled in your hearing.'[17]

From the very start, He identified himself with those at the bottom of the heap.

Those with the 'ears to hear' that Jesus commended would also have recognised that something He said—which is often understood as accepting poverty as just a fact of life—was actually more a statement of resignation than reflection.

For when He told those indignant at the waste of nard poured over His feet by the woman at Simon's house that 'the poor you will always have with you'[18], He observed that they could help out 'any time you want'.[19]

He also appears to have been pointing out that they were sinful in allowing poverty to remain, alluding to the law requiring the cancelling of debts: ' . . . there should be no poor among you, for in the land the Lord your God is giving you to possess as your inheritance, he will richly bless you, if only you fully obey . . . and are careful to follow all these commands . . . '[20]

Eventually Jesus' twin messages of children's value and worth, and the responsibility to care for those in need, did sink in with His disciples, as they watched and listened.

God's Commands about the Poor

Within the early life of the New Testament Church, James was to write reminding the believers that 'Religion that God our Father accepts as pure and faultless is this: to look after orphans and widows in their distress . . . '[21]

In writing so, the author—widely believed to be one of Jesus' brothers—was not only passing on lessons learned from Jesus, but also harking back to a rich scriptural tradition.

For if the culture of Jesus' day was guilty of dismissing or denying the importance of children in God's heart, their standing and significance in His sight—and the need to look out for others less fortunate—was there to be seen by all who would search the religious writings dating back to Moses.

The responsibility of God's people to care for the poor, the oppressed and abandoned children is a clear, recurring theme of the Old Testament—the law which Jesus said He came not to do away with, but to bring to fullness.[22]

God made His care and concern clear from the earliest moments of the Israelites' deliverance from captivity in Egypt, setting among the first laws declared by Moses after he reported the Ten Commandments: 'Do not take advantage of a widow or an orphan. If you do and they cry out to me, I will certainly hear their cry. My anger will be aroused . . . '[23]

But it was not just that the Israelites should not act unfairly to orphans, among others—God wanted them to be proactive, rather than neutral. As a people they had been set apart to show His nature and character to the nations around—and He was one who 'defends the cause of the fatherless and the widow, and loves the alien, giving him food and clothing'.[24]

He didn't just leave it to them to determine how they might do that, but set out clear instructions—for ex-ample, ordering them to leave behind some of the produce of their harvest for the needy to gather.[25] It was these 'gleanings' that Ruth was gathering when she met her future husband, Boaz, in the book of Ruth.

Furthermore, the tithe of their produce that the Israelites were to set aside in the third year of their new life in the Promised Land was to be given to 'the alien, the fatherless and the widow, so that they may eat in your towns and be satisfied'.[26]

The blessings that God promised His people in their new homeland were conditional on their keeping these and the other commands He gave. If they failed to do so, then 'cursed is the man who withholds justice from the alien, the fatherless or the widow'.[27]

There were those who fulfilled God's commands. As, in the midst of his anguish, Job reflected on the blessings of his past life, he recognised that the good standing he enjoyed among his people—a sign of God's favour—was, in part, because of his caring for those in need:

Whoever heard me spoke well of me,
  and those who saw me commended me,
because I rescued the poor who cried for help,
  and the fatherless who had none to assist him . . .

131

I was a father to the needy;
  I took up the case of the stranger.[28]

Affirmed by God Himself as 'blameless and upright',[29] Job saw his practical care for others as much a measure of his integrity as his personal purity:

If I have denied the desires of the poor . . .
if I have kept my bread to myself,
  not sharing it with the fatherless—
but from my youth I reared him as would a father . . . if I have seen anyone perishing for lack of clothing . . . if I have raised my hand against the fatherless,
  knowing that I had influence in court,
then let my arm fall from the shoulder,
  let it be broken off at the joint . . .
  . . . for fear of [God's] splendour I could not do such
    things.[30]

God's heart for the 'fatherless' wasn't left in the Mosaic writings for people to forget, either—the Psalmists reminded them of His compassion, with references to His care and provision throughout their writings.

David and his fellow writers testified that the Lord was 'the helper of the fatherless . . . defending the fatherless and the oppressed'[31]; He was 'a father to the fatherless . . .'[32]; He would repay the wickedness of those who oppress His inheritance, who 'murder the fatherless'[33]; and that, upholding 'the cause of the oppressed', He 'sustains the fatherless'.[34]

But as the Israelites wandered from their loyalty to God, slipping into repeated seasons of idolatry and isolation, they also turned their backs on those in need. Through a succession of prophets God pointed His finger at their spiritual adultery, and also shook His head at their sad failure to look after others.

The immorality for which Sodom is remembered for being judged was actually only part of the story. Specifically, the sin that God considered 'so great . . . so grievous'[35] that He destroyed the city was not her sexual depravity, but her selfishness.

'Now this was the sin of your sister Sodom,' Ezekiel later told the city of Jerusalem at God's direction: 'She and her daughters were arrogant, overfed and unconcerned; they did not help the poor and needy.'[36]

It may be that failure to look after the needs of others leads to an unhealthy preoccupation with one's own needs and desires—and the capacity for increasing self-indulgence—for the prophet adds: 'They were haughty and did detestable things before me. Therefore I did away with them as you have seen.'[37]

When Isaiah stepped forward with his warning of God's impending judgement on Israel, and captivity at the hands of the Babylonians, it was to a nation 'in rebellion'.[38] The sacrifices they made and religious ceremonies they performed were meaningless, he thundered. Their hearts should be measured by their lifestyle, not meaningless rituals:

Stop doing wrong,
   learn to do right!
Seek justice,

encourage the oppressed.
Defend the cause of the fatherless . . . [39]

Next, through Jeremiah, God rebuked His people for failing to 'plead the case of the fatherless',[40] but promising that if they were to change their ways and 'not oppress the alien, the fatherless or the widow . . . then I will let you live in this place, in the land I gave your forefathers for ever and ever'.[41]

The Great Commission

Even apart from this strong thread of the responsibility of God's people to those in need that runs through the Bible, the mandate for Christian involvement in the rejected and runaway children of the world can be found in the Great Commission.

Jesus' final words to His disciples were that they should take the good news of the kingdom of heaven to 'all creation'[42]— which, Doug Nichols observes with some irony almost two millennia later, seems rather unequivocal.

The word of God clearly teaches that we—the Church— should reach everyone with the gospel, whether they are poor or rich, whatever race or level of society, no matter what ethnic background or age, old or young.

Let me paraphrase Paul's words to the church at Colosse, '. . . Christ in you, the hope of glory. And we proclaim him, admonishing every man (which includes street children) and teaching every man (also the ten-year-old child prostitute of Manila, Bangkok or Bogota) with all wisdom, that we may present every man (all street children and underprivileged children throughout the world) complete in Christ'.[43]

Should not this be the purpose of each local church and mission?[44]

With a third of the world's population—1.8 billion people—under the age of fifteen, and 78 per cent of them growing up in non-Christian settings, it is time the Church recognised the significance of reaching young people with the gospel, asserts Bryant Myers.

Calling for the presentation of a 'holistic Christian gospel', he urges: 'The good news of Jesus Christ must be about proclamation and prophecy, the personal and the social, about saving and liberating.

'Many children do not believe adults have any good news . . . .'[45]

Timothy Monsma also believes that it is time the missions world saw that truly working towards the fulfilling of the Great Commission will involve recognising street children as an 'unreached people group'.

'From the point of view of those who work in cities, it is a mistake to neglect prominent social groupings while concentrating only on ethnic groups,' he maintains.[46]

'If street children are a prominent unreached people group in cities, here is a group with millions of souls that has not yet been seriously addressed with the gospel.'[47]

CHAPTER TEN

THE RESCUERS

*' . . . gave . . . with such kind and gentle
words, and with such tears of
sympathy and compassion . . .'*

OLIVER TWIST: CHAPTER EIGHT

The House of Restoration

AM I a person?' It was one of the strangest and most
poignant questions Johan Lukasse had ever heard,
asked by a nine-year-old boy who came to the day-
time drop-in house which offers street kids a shower and some
food.

'It really intrigued me, and I asked him why he wanted to
know. He said because people called him "garbage", and all
kinds of other names . . .'

The same question is repeated, in different style, each time
Lukasse visits the streets with his co-workers. They are sur-
rounded by a crowd of excitable boys, all reaching out wanting to shake hands.

Lukasse makes sure he greets each child by name, taking
their hand and touching the back of their head or neck affec-
tionately as he talks with them. They lap up the attention.

'The street kids have huge emotional needs, they really want someone to recognise them as a person, with value. They crave attention,' he observes.

In the decade that he and his wife, Jeannette, have led a Youth With A Mission ministry to street children in Belo Horizonte, Brazil's fourth largest city, he has become a well-known and well-loved figure among the street children.

The couple have also won the respect of community and church leaders, who have seen the work grow to include a day centre, two halfway houses, a home specifically for children with AIDS, and a daily feeding programme.

While others wring their hands at the scale of the street children problem, the Lukasses—like others in cities of the world—are quietly rolling up their sleeves and reaching into the mess of their streets to help.

They work on the streets—tending wounds, handing out meals, making bridges of trust a cautious span at a time. They work in hostels and drop-in centres, where the youngsters can take their first tentative steps away from the pavements.

Others take a step back from the streets, turning to the slum communities where family breakdown and pressures force children out of the home, to try to stem the tide of 'runaways and throwaways' by helping families stay together.

That could be anything from supporting simple wage-earning initiatives to family counselling.

Meanwhile government-sponsored 'street educators'— many former street kids themselves—look for ways of helping the youngsters survive better where they are, offering health advice and even reading programmes.

They all recognise that 'the young cannot wait for global problems to be solved to receive the attention and care necessary for their survival. Their needs are immediate'.[1]

The Lukasses—he a former school teacher, she a trained nurse—have seen just about everything through the years. One day a six-year-old boy ran into the kitchen and snatched a knife to protect himself from one of the others.

They have met nine-year-olds who have admitted murdering other kids. One night a thirteen-year-old girl arrived looking for help and they took her in—only to discover later that she was the killer of a street boy whose funeral they were arranging.

Another time they had to go to the rescue of a sixteen-year-old girl who was being chased by her former gang, angry that she had drawn police attention to them.

Sick through years of cocaine use, she was in hospital when the gang arrived, carrying guns. They grabbed a nurse at gunpoint and made her take them to the girl, but the police were called just in time.

When she arrived at the Lukasses' House of Restoration, they knew that her years of prostituting herself to feed her habit had exacted a high toll. She had AIDS.

Along the way the phlegmatic Dutch couple have also adopted two children alongside their three own, a handicapped boy and girl. And they have been threatened and robbed by some of the youngsters they have been trying to help.

What keeps them going is 'more an anger than just a compassion', says Johan. 'It's not that I am always stirred in my heart and feeling as if I want to cry. Sometimes I do if I am praying—I will suddenly get a sense of God's heart for them—but it is not really just to do with feeling.

'When I am out on the streets it's more that I get angry at the enemy, Satan, who is trying to rob and kill the kids. It gives me a determination to go on with the job, to really do something about it.'

The Happy Child Mission

Shortly after becoming a Christian, Sarah Jarman was praying for Brazil and saw the strangest scene in her mind's eye: the Pied Piper with lots of children on the street dancing. God told her: 'You are the Pied Piper.'

Baffled and unaware of Brazil's street children problem, she began asking around—'and somebody said to me, "Don't you know that there are many street children who are dying and being killed?" And I knew then that I couldn't stay. I had to go'.

Turning her back on a lucrative publicity and producer's career in TV and film—where her credits included the films *Greystoke* and *The Killing Fields*—she joined YWAM as one of their unpaid volunteers.

But her first exposure to the Brazilian streets was almost too much. 'After two weeks of seeing kids dead or sleeping out, or fighting, or so drugged that they were knocked down by cars as they crossed the road, I remember thinking, "This is hopeless. What am I doing here. I want to go home. It's such an enormous problem, what can I do?" '

In the middle of her crisis she met a 'very sweet and kind' eighteen-year-old. 'He said that he had been a street kid for fourteen years. I was amazed—about a third of them die before they reach his age.

'As I heard him tell me he had become a Christian through the love of some missionaries, I thought, "That's why I am here". And I scrapped all my longings to go back to my comfortable job.'

After working in some of Rio de Janeiro's most infamous *favelas*—shanty towns of which there are more than 700 thrown up around the city—she started a new ministry with her new Brazilian husband, John.

Together they have founded the Happy Child Mission, based on a farm on the outskirts of Belo Horizonte, to which they bring boys and girls from the streets for a time to 'heal and be restored'.

From there they are placed with adoptive Christian families.

Bob Sanchez

Things were going well for Bob Sanchez and the small church he was pastoring in the university area of Manila. They offered hostel accommodation for some of the students, which proved to be a good link between the young people and the congregation.

But then he became aware of the street boys hanging around even the church's middle-income area. 'We realised that we could not just ignore what was going on around us,' recalls the ever-smiling leader. 'We couldn't just hold worship services and Bible studies and prayer meetings while people were suffering. It would be completely pretentious.

'When you really study the Scriptures, you discover that Jesus Christ, when He did His ministry, He didn't just "preach the gospel". When He approached a person He saw them in their entirety; He looked at them and first found their need, and ministered to that. Then He shared the gospel.

'Take the example of the ten lepers. They all got healed, although only one of them returned to be saved.'

Now the church runs a low-key drop-in centre where street kids can come for a wash, some medical attention and some food. After a time they are invited to join one of the residential programmes, where boys will be taken into a hostel and taught some work skills.

With help from overseas funding, the church provides instructors to teach candlemaking. They also show them how to weave wicker-style baskets out of shredded telephone directories and old copies of *Time* magazine.

Some of the church members were sceptical at first. 'They said that the boys would steal from us, and we did have some of those experiences,' he recalls.

But members are now used to some of the scruffily dressed youngsters joining them for the Sunday service, and many volunteer as temporary foster parents at Christmas and other holidays, when they take boys in from the shelter to their homes.

Central to their approach is Bible study and encouraging the street kids to grow as Christians. 'We believe that Jesus is the answer, because there must be a transformation inside, rather than the behavioural idea that you just need to change the external environment.

'That can help, yes, but essentially what is needed is a change of heart. Then all the other external things can become helpful.'

Loreto School and the Rainbow Students

Sister Cyril retains a slightly ruddy Irish complexion despite nearly forty years in India, and a hearty, caring but no-nononsense disposition summed up by her belief that: 'Problems are things to be solved, not wept over.'

She also has one of the grubbiest collections of stuffed animals ever to be seen, making a soft mini-mountain in her small principal's office at Loreto School, just across the street from Calcutta's Sealdah railway station.

The giant koala bear and other toys gather their grime from the street children who wander at will into the office, interrupting Sister Cyril's paperwork, for a hug from her and a squeeze with them before disappearing again.

She is unfazed by a series of brief such 'visits', pausing only to observe that 'it isn't enough to go out and do social work, because you leave the people behind when you come back. You have to invite them in, and so you have to accept that means they will disturb you and the place won't be so marvellously clean and tidy.

'That's just the price you pay, but the children are far more important than the appearance of my office'.

Disturbed by the vast numbers of young children working

and living on the streets around and at the station—the city's second largest—the Dublin-born nun decided to do her 'little bit', and enlisted the help of the rest of the school . . .

The uniformed pupils go over to the station to make friends with some of the hundreds of children who sleep nearby, making money by running errands or begging or stealing. Then they invite them to the school.

The street kids are welcome to drop in whenever they can, recognising that many have to work to support themselves and their families. There will be some food and also the chance to learn some reading and writing or handicrafts from one of the older, full-time pupils through the school's 'each one reach one' policy.

Some of the fee-paying parents were a little aghast at first at what might happen to their nice Catholic school, Sister Cyril admits, and the free-and-easy approach does require 'some flexibility'.

'If poor children can't feel at home, then change your school because the school is wrong, not the child. The street child should be the most important one because they are the most deprived,' she asserts, adding that the programme has over the years become widely accepted by pupils and parents.

Helping the Rainbow students—the full-time pupils decided they needed a nicer name than 'street kids' and chose one reflecting different colours of creation—is 'a tremendously formative experience'.

A small island in Calcutta's—and India's—sea of problems and poverty, Sister Cyril refuses to be overwhelmed. 'Children are the future of the country. We are here for them and therefore I can't rest until everyone has access to good food and education.

'Then all the other problems will start to solve themselves. If we develop people, they will develop the resources needed to deal with everything else. Sadly governments often develop the resources, but forget to develop the people along with them.'

As well as looking to the street kids' futures, Sister Cyril offers practical help for their present-day realities: self-defence lessons. 'It helps them to protect themselves, and gives them some sense of self-respect, worth. That gets totally destroyed—they feel they are dirty nobodies.'

Children of the Andes Foundation

Concern for street children and a commitment to help them isn't restricted to biblically-motivated Christians, as Ana Vascencelos' work in Brazil highlights. Nor is she alone.

Colombian businessman Jaime Jaramillo has won international acclaim for his work with the Children of the Andes Foundation he launched after a chance encounter one Christmas over twenty years ago.

Walking in Bogota, he happened to notice a young street girl dash out into the road to scoop a toy box thrown from a passing car. As she did she was struck by a truck and killed— and when Jaramillo went to her aid he discovered that the box was empty. He was appalled and angered by the waste of a life. Starting to visit the street kids regularly, he took food, clothing and medical supplies.

When he asked one girl where she lived, he was surprised at the address she gave—in a street in a fashionable part of the city.

It turned out that she meant underground—where she and a group of other children made a home of sorts in the dark sewers, amid the waste and rats.

Creeping through the foul tunnels while making a programme about Jaramillo's work, veteran British TV journalist Desmond Wilcox observed, 'In thirty years of making documentary films around the world from typhoons to war zones to personal tragedies . . . this is probably the most horrendous location I have ever been in.'

Jaramillo continues to visit the sewers regularly, in diving gear—once finding a fifteen-year-old girl giving birth on a ledge just above the putrid waters.

After befriending them, he invites them to join one of the halfway houses the foundation now runs.

'I cannot give up,' he explained. 'When you have 300 kids in the homes to help and thousands more back on the streets, you cannot go back. Whatever happens, I have to keep going.'[2]

Future Hope

When top British banker Tim Grandidge discovered a group of boys living on the pavement outside his offices in Calcutta, he made them a deal: 'You look after my car, and I will look after you.'

After a while he built a shelter on the roof of his apartment building, somewhere the boys could stay for the night. Then his bank told him they wanted him to transfer to Hong Kong—and he decided to give up his job, devoting himself full-time to his Future Hope project.

Even with several homes, run by Indian house parents and where boys can stay and receive educational and vocational training, it is not even really beginning to scratch the surface of the needs of the city.

'The problem is so huge that something would have to be done on a macro-level, but in India that is not possible at present—economically or culturally,' said co-worker Martin Graham. 'So in the meantime, we do what we can.

'If we can make one difference for one child for even one day, that's worth it. You know that when you talk with the children or hold their hands, or have them trust you with their few rupees . . .'

Among those who helps raise funds for Future Hope is top Indian actor Om Puri—who starred in the film version of *City of Joy*, chronicling some of Calcutta's crushing poverty.

The Holly Ryder Foundation

Meanwhile, in the United States, former leading porn film star Lisa Marie Abato recently began campaigning for X-rated movies to be declared a form of prostitution—leading to tighter legal controls—in an effort to protect young runaways from being lured into the industry.[3]

After leaving the porn industry in 1992, she founded the Holly Ryder Foundation—the title coming from her screen name in over 200 blue films—to help the teenagers she says are recruited from the streets of Hollywood.

Running away from an abusive home at thirteen she moved to California and later had filmed sex for three years. 'When you have low self-esteem, it is very hard to get beyond that,' she said.[4]

Jubilee Action

The offices just a cheer's distance away behind the stand of Wimbledon Football Club's pitch in southwest London seem a long way from the streets of South America, but for a long time they were the centre of efforts to help street children there.

Although not obviously at the 'sharp end' it was here in make-do offices crammed with research documents and reports that Danny Smith and his human rights Jubilee Action team concentrated their efforts to see changes in attitudes, actions and law relating to street children.

The UK campaigners—more recently moved to more suitable facilities—have played a major behind-the-scenes role in seeing street children become a political issue in recent years.

Through tireless lobbying they encouraged the founding of an all-party group of MPs committed to pursuing the issue at an international level, asking questions in Parliament about human rights abuses.

They also played a key part in the recently-launched Consortium for Street Children umbrella group, which has brought together a wide range of campaign and charitable organisations, and also funnels money to groups running centres and street kid projects.

But their focus is 'the big picture'. 'Change won't come overnight,' says Smith, 'but we are in this for the long haul.'

Opening Hearts and Homes

Top basketball coach **Pat Williams and his wife, Jill,** decided they could do something to help street children in the Philippines and Brazil from their home in Orlando, Florida.

Or, more accurately, *in* it.

They adopted five street children from the two countries, taking their family of natural and adopted children to eighteen.

One visiting journalist observed that their home 'may look appropriately middle-class, but inside it's clear they've sacrificed personal peace and affluence for a commitment to give abandoned children from around the world a new life'.[5]

The couple explain: 'There are forty-one references in the Bible to God's special concern for orphans . . . we simply responded to a need.'

Things do not always turn out so picture perfect. Missionaries **David and Rachel Perkins** decided to adopt seven-year-old **Jose** when they befriended him in Manila and were told by a doctor that without committed help his life expectancy was another couple of years at most.

They took him home to America with high hopes, helping him learn both the strange new culture and also the basics like eating from a plate and sleeping in a bed at night—both strange to a 'monkey-like' little boy used to feeding himself with his fingers and sleeping in snatched catnaps.

As he adapted, it became clearer that there were more serious problems. His years of severe neglect and malnourishment had left him physically stunted, with damaged eyesight and hearing, and retarded. That meant large medical bills—not the only price to be paid.

Emotionally he had been scarred, too, leaving him unable to really feel or seem a close part of the family. Prayer and counselling haven't changed things.

'We have learned to adjust our expectations,' they admit candidly. 'For Jose we are happy; if we hadn't adopted him, he probably wouldn't be alive today.

'But for ourselves, our marriage and our other children, if we were to go back in time I am not sure that we would do the same thing again.'

The Cost of Caring

The Perkins are not the only ones to have ever questioned. Even recognising that young broken lives don't get put together overnight, the long and slow journey from the streets to a new life can exact a heavy toll on those working with the young people.

'It's one of the major issues our workers struggle with in terms of spiritual warfare, just keeping going,' says Johan Lukasse. 'Because of the time involved, and the lack of results you see. It's easy to get discouraged.'

Psychologist Anne Balfour believes that for some street children, the familiarity of what they know—however difficult— is to be preferred to an unknown future away from the streets.

'It's typical of a person with psychological problems—the abused person who marries an abuser. Somehow it seems safer to stay with what you know, however bad.'

She recalled **Maria**, a Colombian girl in her early teens who attended a drop-in centre for some time but then disappeared. The workers were concerned for her safety, and relieved when she reappeared a few weeks later—but only, it turned out, to collect the things she had left at the centre, and return to the streets with her boyfriend.

'She found it very difficult to accept love and friendship, and people caring for her. It was almost as if it was too much, she was scared . . . It just showed what a narrow line there is in bringing kids off the streets. It's a slow process that can take years.'

Edson was the leader of one of the first gangs the Lukasses came into contact with when they ventured out onto the streets. They were surprised when, within a short time, he and his group all decided they wanted to become Christians, leave the streets, and start over.

Edson even completed a six-month Discipleship Training School, a Youth With A Mission programme which helps Christians grow in their faith and prepare for missionary service.

But then he went back to his home area for a visit, and failed to return. Soon he was back in his old ways, running the streets. The last they heard of him he was living back at home with his mother and stepfather—for the time being, at least.

'It was really disappointing, but there was really not much more we could have done for him,' Johan reflects. 'At a certain point they really have to make a choice; he consciously made a choice to disobey God, while knowing that he shouldn't.

'The street itself is an addiction stronger than any drug they use there. They need a lot more rehabilitation to get that out of their hearts and systems than the desire for drugs.

'I don't think that it takes anything less than a real miracle of the Holy Spirit in their lives. They might even change their habits for a little, but if they don't have a change of heart they will be the same person, basically, even if they have cleaned themselves up and have a job.'

It's this perspective that separates Christian-based street children programmes from many others—the recognition that even 'innocent victims' of abuse and abandonment are, according to Scripture, sinners in need of repentance and a new life.

It is a delicate job balancing compassion for the street kids' plight with confrontation of their own wrong-doing, recognising that while desperate circumstances may push many of them unwillingly into a life of crime, wrong is still wrong.

'We need to look at sin from God's perspective. Our human tendency is often to make the problem and the sin bigger than God's ability to heal or set them free,' reflects Joe Appler, who for several years directed the Centrum House and Homes of Hope programmes which reached out to youngsters drawn to Hollywood.

Attracted by dreams of rubbing shoulders with film greats and being 'discovered', very soon would-be stars and starlets find themselves instead selling their bodies for something to eat.

'It's a contradiction, because I see them as a victim and a victimiser. My heart goes out to them. They are growing up in a messed-up world.

'You can't save or sanctify the flesh, and I really believe that no matter how many contributing reasons there were for their running away from the home, their problem there on the street is the flesh. They want to live to gratify themselves.

'Of course many of them have good reason to leave home— but no good reason to gratify the flesh. I don't feel sorry for them; I am moved to compassion. I don't say "poor kids".

'It doesn't mean I may not be moved and weep, and persevere with their background and touch heaven for them. But even the most abused of us will get to stand before God and be judged. And I don't want that to happen. I want them to be forgiven.'

CHAPTER ELEVEN

WHEN LOVE BREAKS THROUGH

' . . . think how changed he is . . .'

OLIVER TWIST: CHAPTER FIFTY-ONE

Larry

LIKE MANY BOYS, when Larry San Pedro was young his dream was to become a military officer.

So he could kill his father easily.

'I promised myself that I would kill him because I never felt his love and concern for me,' he recalled.[1]

'He always beat me. Sometimes he used chains or a stool. He even poked a knife at me just because I was not able to fetch water for the family use . . . He would beat me without any reason.'

By the time he was five, Larry had taken to sleeping out with a group of street boys, curling up in parked jeepneys— the brightly decorated cannibalised jeeps, part bus, part taxi, that almost constantly circle Manila's crowded streets, pouring out fumes.

Once a friend was stabbed and killed during the night while Larry slept unawares nearby.

Selling newspapers and cigarettes during the day, washing jeepneys—working early before school and late into the night

155

afterwards—he made enough money to help support his mother, and keep a little for himself.

When he was seven he visited a Sunday school where someone told him that Jesus loved the street children. Larry prayed to come to know this God as his friend—but it didn't take away the anger in his heart.

'I tried to take drugs, sniff glue and solvent, drink liquor and join the bad boys in our place to get away from this bitterness. But it didn't help me, I only became more bitter . . .'[2]

But then when he was eleven, he attended a holiday Bible club where he was 'moved by the Holy Spirit to forgive my father and love him instead'—and he realised he had changed.

Since then, Larry has trained as a pastor, regularly returning to the streets to tell youngsters living as he had about the love of God.

Jorge

His years in the 'concrete' jungle turned out to be a sort of rugged apprenticeship for Jorge's new life in the real one.

The young Brazilian swapped the crowded streets of Belo Horizonte for the thick undergrowth of the Amazon rainforest, after turning his back on years of gang life.

Running away from a violent home at the age of five, he soon found himself caught up with one of the city's clusters of street children, begging or stealing from passers-by and regularly sniffing glue to squash his feelings of loneliness.

Violence was never far away. One time he saw members of

a rival gang burned to death. He lost a finger after thrusting his hand into a fan while high on glue.

After seven years it seemed only a matter of time before Jorge would become just another statistic.

And then he came into contact with a group who ran a day-time drop-in centre where street kids could get a shower, a hot meal, and watch some TV before heading out to the pavements and gutters again.

In time the words of the Youth With A Mission workers got through to him; there was more to life than he had. God loved him and cared for him, and could help him change.

Jorge decided to try their rehabilitation centre, but it wasn't easy. The rules, the emphasis on God, the need to start taking personal responsibility all seemed a bit stifling.

He would try to follow the system for a while, but just find it too much, and end up back on the streets. Only there he would soon realise again the harsh reality of life—and death—there.

Finally he realised he needed to break the spiral. At seventeen he went back to the YWAM house one more time, asking for one more chance to make a go of things. They agreed—and this time Jorge made it.

On 'graduating' from the YWAM centre he decided to take a special training school for new workers with the organisation—for, he told staff, God had called him to take the gospel to a small tribe in the Amazon jungle.

'I know this is why God raised me out of the streets,' he said as he set out for the jungle with his new wife, and a third YWAM colleague.

Jorge's ability to fend for himself, honed on the unfriendly streets, stood him and his team in good stead, as they faced malaria and had to hunt for their food while they searched for the hidden Rimariman Indians.

Among his prayer supporters in his new missionary life are the Lukasses and their YWAM team back in Belo. 'With all the desperate and despairing children we see, it is wonderful to have a success story like this. It shows us that God loves these children and wants to use them to serve Him.'

Jennifer

While a handshake with Jorge would reveal the scars that have to heal as street lives are turned around, not all are so visible.

Sitting in a coffee shop in a fashionable Manila shopping centre, Jennifer looked as though she could have stepped down from one of the advertising hoardings along the nearby stores. Attractive and well dressed, the dark-haired young woman seemed a world away from the city's rougher streets— but told how, even with them well behind, her homeless years were still a significant part of her.

For almost four years, Jennifer made her home on the streets with her mother, who would sell sex to make a few coins, while her little daughter slept fitfully nearby.

At other times she would send Jennifer out to beg, her childish good looks drawing sympathy and support from passers-by in the tourist streets, or door to door in some of the richer neighbourhoods.

But not always. 'Some days we wouldn't get anything at all.

We would just get turned down all day long, and have to depend on picking bread up off the street,' she recalled.

They slept 'just about everywhere', and even now travelling around the city she will suddenly remember a street corner or bridge from her child's viewpoint.

Vacant buildings were favourite sleeping places, dry and warm. Settling down close to a church also reduced the likelihood of being moved on by the police.

Things started to go wrong when her mother became pregnant again, although Jennifer was attached to her. Suddenly the woman would swing between affection and anger, lashing out for no reason.

When her mother went into hospital to give birth, Jennifer found herself taken to a Christian-run orphanage. Though she had somehow survived all her years on the streets without being harmed, within a short time in the home she was abused by one of the other children.

When an American missionary family began to take an interest in her and visit her, it made things worse. They would take along gifts, which the other children would steal once they had left.

Yet despite her confused feelings Jennifer warmed to the kind couple and their children, and eventually went to live with them. The family adopted her, taking her with them for assignments in England and the US before returning to the Philippines.

Although she prayed to become a Christian at the age of about seven, Jennifer's teenage years found her confused and rebellious.

Her features and complexion made it clear she was different from the rest of the family, which often led to insensitive questions from others.

'I rebelled, but it was all internal. People wouldn't really see it. I would look happy, I was popular, but no one really knew about my past.

'Once when we were visiting a church I tried to share with the group of young people because they had asked why I was adopted, so I told them but then they didn't know what to say . . .'

Having parents whom everyone else thought were wonderful for 'taking her in' didn't help with her confusion—feeling guilty for not feeling grateful. 'I sort of disassociated myself from the family, and then later had to learn to try to fit in with them.'

At twenty, doing well in school and rediscovering her faith, Jennifer found herself coming to terms with her past, and even able to offer her own experiences to help others.

'For a long time when I saw beggars and street people I would shun them, try to ignore them. But then I started to have a real compassion for them. I joined a street ministry and shared my testimony with some of the street kids.'

She was also able to draw on her own experiences to act as on-the-set adviser for a Christian film dramatising the life of street children, bringing the reality of their situation and needs to church and family audiences.

For a long time she 'wished life had been different'. 'But eventually I gave up on that. This is the way God planned my life, even if I don't understand some of the stuff that happened—I have to accept that and move on from there.'

Marlon

Like Jennifer, as Marlon grows as a Christian he is able to acknowledge that 'the pain and suffering that mark my heart are fading'.[3]

The smiling young man returns often to share the love of God on the streets that very nearly claimed his life.

He arrived in Manila alone at the age of eight, leaving behind an unhappy home where his stepfather had tried to stab him in a drunken rage.

Young and impressionable, he thought his luck had changed when a kindly man approached offering to help. The foreigner took Marlon back to his hotel room and molested him. Back on the streets, drugs helped numb the pain. Soon he was using them regularly, and started acting as a youthful pimp, selling girls to tourists, to make enough money.

Arrested and sent to a juvenile rehabilitation centre, he was out six months later—wiser, but tougher, and at twelve ready to join a serious crime gang, mixing drugs, theft and armed holdups.

It was not long before their notoriety saw them targeted for 'salvaging'—the local term for killing—and Marlon was arrested with two of his friends.

Taken to a secluded part of the city, away from potential witnesses, the young boy watched in horror as the police gouged out his two friends' eyes and then pumped their bodies full of bullets.[4]

Turning to Marlon, they clubbed him with a gun, hand-cuffed him and tied him to the back of their car. It seemed that death was only moments away, but somehow he managed to work free and run away, as bullets flew around him.

Some time later, he passed a group of 'different-looking' people on the street. They were from Christ for Greater Manila, Christians sharing the gospel with streets kids in the city.

Marlon responded to the message he heard, moving in to the group's rescue centre. But the change was hard. He ran away fifteen times before finally deciding to make a real go of his new Christian life.

After two years at the group's rehabilitation home outside Manila, Marlon returned to school and became a regular volunteer at CGM outreaches and street kids camps, sharing his testimony as an example of how God can change lives.

Tono and Pradip

The grim reality and dark detail Marlon shares, along with many others, makes his testimony of a new heart and a fresh start too bruising to be called 'storybook' or 'fairytale', but it underscores God's ability to rescue the all-too-lost little ones.

Like Tono. The scar still marks his face from where he was slashed by another street boy, but it's the smile you notice most in the photographs.

The ACTION missionaries came across him on the streets of Bogota soon after he had been wounded, offering first aid and seeing he got the medical treatment he needed.

He had never really enjoyed the dangers and dirt, and when they offered him the chance of a clean start he jumped at it. Now he is living with a Christian family, transformed from 'a dirty, ragged, tense, glue-sniffing street boy . . . into a clean, inquisitive, relaxed, friendly and courteous young man'.[5]

For Pradip, his six miserable years at Calcutta's Howrah station—he fled there after his mother died—seem 'a bit like a dream. No, a nightmare', as he now studies in school at a Christian orphanage.

'So many boys there; why did God choose me, I ask? I want to become a pastor and to help some of my brothers back at the station. You have to remember where you came from, by the grace of God.'

CHAPTER TWELVE

THE TUG OF WAR . . .

'. . . I dream so much of Heaven,
and Angels, and kind faces
that I never see when I am awake . . .'

OLIVER TWIST: CHAPTER SEVEN

IT SHOULD NOT really be so surprising that God might use fiction to reawaken His people to some overlooked facts.

After all, the Bible is full of His reconciling apparent opposites in the establishing of His Kingdom. A virgin giving birth to a baby. Swords into ploughshares. The first become last.

Which may be how a potboiling novel about angels and demons doing battle over the souls of a small American town came to do more than any number of 'serious' books on the subject in stirring a renewed awareness of the importance of spiritual warfare.

Frank Peretti's *This Present Darkness* and its sequel *Piercing the Darkness* may not have had all their theological commas in exactly the right places, but their broad sweep stirred Christians' hearts and minds.

Churches across all kinds of denominational boundaries around the world took on board in a new way the seriousness of the spiritual battle which the Bible says rages all around.

They may still disagree on the finer points of how that should be applied and incorporated, but generally speaking many Christians have embraced in a new way their responsibility to be active and effective in the unseen world about us.

And it could just be, too, that there is something similar to be found in the story of Oliver Twist—beyond even the essential parable of a child being denied his rightful inheritance, the discovery of which preceded this book's research.

A Face at the Window

For a closer study of Dickens' text reveals that the plot to rob young Oliver of what was rightly his and share the spoils was hatched between the street kids' 'director', Fagin—also known as 'the Jew' and 'the merry old gentleman'—and one Monks, Oliver's villainous half-brother.

After various adventures with the Artful Dodger and other members of the gang, Oliver is taken pity on by the prostitute Nancy, who smuggles him away from Fagin's lair to a safe house.

Later he is taken into the country by his kind benefactors, far from the scenes of his crimes. And one evening, as he dozes by the window . . .

Suddenly, the scene changed; the air become close and confined; and he thought, with a glow of terror, that he was in the Jew's house again. There sat the hideous old man, in his accustomed corner, pointing at him and whispering to another man, with his face averted, who sat beside him.

'Hush, my dear!' he thought he heard the Jew say; 'it is he, sure enough. Come away.'[1]

Oliver wakes with a start.

Good God! what was that, which sent the blood tingling to his heart, and deprived him of his voice, and of power to move! There—there—at the window—close before him—so close, that he could have almost touched him before he started back: with his eyes peering into the room, and meeting his: there stood the Jew![2]

Alerted by Oliver's cries, the others in the house rush outside, but search as they might there is no sign of the two men anywhere.

The search was all in vain. There were not even the traces of recent footsteps to be seen . . . 'It must have been a dream, Oliver,' said Harry Maylie.
'Oh no, indeed, sir,' replied Oliver, shuddering at the very recollection of the old wretch's countenance; 'I saw him too plainly for that . . . '.[3]

This seemingly rather obscure episode becomes more interesting in the light of comments on the classic by scholar Angus Wilson, who refers to the 'certain supernatural element implied in the diabolic character of Fagin, and the mysterious absence of his footprints after he has peered in upon Oliver in his country retreat, and in the whole phantom character of Monks'.[4]
Observing that 'Fagin, the "merry old gentleman" '—a term

commonly used to refer to the devil—is 'an extraordinary compound of the supernatural, extreme realism, and macabre humour', he refers to the 'sense of pervasive evil' embodied in the character.

Furthermore, with Fagin 'is associated the humour and fun of the criminal life, but, unlike Dodger's cockney toughness, his humour is wholly horrible, his games invented to corrupt the boys . . .'[5]

Noting that Fagin's appearance at the window portrays 'a nightmare effect of a net enclosing Oliver wherever he may be', he concludes: 'Here is indeed the "merry old gentleman", the devil; beside him the epileptic wandering figure of Monks seems but a feeble attendant demon.'[6]

Spiritual Warfare in Brazil

These interesting—but let us be clear, literary, not theological—comments did seem to take on a deeper significance, though, following a visit to the Lukasses' House of Restoration.

Johan spoke of the struggles, the ups and downs, the two-paces-forward-and-then-three-back nature of working with the street kids as they swung from a desire to get away from the gutters, to enjoying every moment there—or at least saying that they did.

'There's a lot of patience involved in reaching out to them,' he observed. 'But one of the things I am aware of is the strong spiritual warfare that's involved in the lives of these young kids. There is a real bondage involved.'

Then he added, unprompted: 'It's really interesting, you know, over the years I have heard this story told back to me time and again, whether from the kids themselves or our workers in the programme . . .

'There comes a certain point when they have been with us when they say that someone will appear to them in front of the window and beckon with their hand, saying, "Come, come . . ." It's somebody asking them to go out into the streets . . .

'I have come to the conclusion with some of the others here that there definitely seems to be some kind of manifestation of an evil spirit that calls them to go back to the street. I have heard the story too often for it to be a coincidence, as far as I am concerned.

'Usually, apparently, it is a nice white person—they associate that with dignity and good standing in Brazil—or somebody robed in white. One of the boys we took to church yesterday said that it happened to him there.

'I definitely believe that it is to do with a stronghold in the lives of these children, and in this whole thing of having been in the streets, and being involved in stealing, prostitution and drugs. We believe it is in fact a destructive force aimed at a whole generation here.'

It is a viewpoint shared by many involved in similar ministries.'There's no question that these children not only need physical and emotional help, but also spiritual deliverance,' say John and Sarah de Carvalho.

'Only the name of Jesus can do that, replacing the hate and violence with His unconditional love. Both of us have witnessed this happening in many of the street children's lives, with our own eyes.

'Many of them live in the most terrible situations, where maybe their parents are drinking too much, or they are part of a family where they don't get any love, perhaps they are even abused, and they go to the streets looking for freedom.

'But they only find a false freedom there. I think of the verse in the Bible which talks about the enemy coming to kill, destroy and steal, and that is how Satan works with these children.

'They need a time when they can be healed emotionally and physically.'

Edmeia Williams, who also works with street children from Brazil's slums, is equally convinced that for all that can be done practically to help the youngsters reform, it's the prayer dimension that makes the difference.

'The wife of a government minister opened three houses, but the girls leave at night and go out to work as prostitutes,' she said.[7]

'The Christian children do not go back to drugs, witchcraft and prostitution. It is the only thing that makes a difference.'

. . . in Calcutta

Premila Pavamani and her husband, Vijayan, run a school and orphanage for street children in Calcutta, the city named after the Hindu goddess of destruction, where blood sacrifices are offered regularly in countless shrines.

From their years of work, they are persuaded that prayer

is a vital, integral part of ministry, alongside the practical.

'It's never enough to just help them,' says this seemingly tireless school manager, teacher, counsellor and friend. 'All these kids from the streets are so scarred from being hurt by people and different situations that they will never be able to be fulfilled human beings apart from Jesus, who can heal them,' she commented.

'We don't go into detail with them over the hurts they have suffered in their lives, because we feel that can just make them more aware about things, but we pray and trust God to lead them and wipe away their tears.

'So many of them go back to the streets—it's like a drug. It's an addiction that has to be broken.'

Vijayan believes that 'Christian discipleship . . . is one of the most important therapies' in rehabilitation: 'The weapon of prayer has achieved much where the best methodology has proved inadequate.'[8]

. . . in South America

Researcher Patrick McDonald noted the particular power of the gospel in reaching street children, during a 15,000-mile, seventeen-city tour of projects throughout South America.

He was 'stunned' to discover the 'obvious difference in success between the Christian and secular organisations'.[9]

'Whereas the secular, humanistic projects were run by trained professionals, skilled staff and often good funding, the Christian projects were often run by mere amateurs in comparison.

'However, the results of the Christians were better to such an extent that conclusions must be drawn,' he noted, citing one secular project in San Salvador where only two kids had left the streets after ten years of work.

'The difficulties of the lives of many of these kids require answers very few people can give without the truth of the gospel.'

. . . in Bombay

The plush Taj Mahal Hotel stretches up alongside the historic Gateway to India in Bombay, 'modern Raj' in its opulence, with the luxurious Presidential Suites liable to set you back around £500 a night.

Just across the road and round the corner is the beginnings of a red-light district where women and young girls will sell themselves for less than the price of a tube of Taj toothpaste.

On the corner between the hotel and the sex-for-sale sidestreets is Bowen Memorial Methodist Church, dating back a century. Here, each Sunday night, Ivan Raskino gathers as many of the street families from around the area he can, and tells them about Jesus.

A former sailor and businessman, he now pastors a 'middle-class' church in another part of the city, and brings members along each week to help him reach out to the street people. They hold a short open-air service on the steps of the church before inviting those interested inside.

There are rich pickings for the begging street children in the area, because of all the wealthy tourists. Some of the youngsters have even learned to speak a few words of Italian and French, which impresses a few more rupees out of the passers-by.

But despite the comparative success of the youngsters — certainly against the thousands of others scrabbling for survival in the vast city—Raskino still sees spiritual forces at work, that need to be addressed.

'How does it affect you as a child when you see your mother molested by a policeman, or raped? Your dad beaten up? You can only get over that by the power of God; He has got to heal your broken heart,' he contends.

'I prayed for a long time about this, and began to see the spiritual forces at work here, I believe. I have identified them as the spirits of lawlessness and hopelessness. I believe that they are the key because they work in terms of human degradation, and the evil one wants nothing more than to rub the noses of human beings made in the image of God into the ground.'

. . . in Manila

Recognising the spiritual dynamic of their work, missionaries in Manila made a point of asking young people about their experiences with the supernatural, in a detailed survey they carried out.

They found many of the respondents telling of 'strange or unexplained phenomena', having heard about or seen demons and *maligno*—evil spirits, ghosts or 'white ladies'—traditional Filipino apparitions.[10] These entities were cited as the cause of as much fear among the street boys as the visible threats they faced from drunks, addicts and police.

'The presence of spiritual-related practitioners and the spiritual beings as reported by some of the respondents are indications that there are some demonic activities or presences controlling or securing the area [where the street children live]', concluded the report.[11]

'Territorial spirits are not directly mentioned, but the ways in which the children and their families are oppressed and harassed by some invisible spiritual forces, are enough proof of demonic presence.'

The street kids' ignorance about God and Jesus Christ was 'further aggravated by the domination of the spirit beings and spirit-related practitioners', it went on. 'For Christians, spiritual warfare is real, not imaginary, when doing ministry to street children.' Local churches wanting to reach out to street children 'should recognise the presence and reality of the demons and the spirit world', said the authors.

An accompanying report surveying young people following a residential Christian-based rehabilitation programme warned that home staff 'cannot afford to downplay or dismiss' the area of prayer and spiritual warfare. It urged:

Regular times of 'spiritual warfare' praying, accompanied with fasting, need to be employed. The evil spirits and influences brought into the home from the street should require a regular cleansing in the power of the Holy Spirit.

However, as in everything, balance is needed. Every antisocial or anti-God statement, or even the behaviour of the boys, cannot be attributed to the evil one. Moderation, dis-

cernment, balance and caution should be the watchword . . .
Any work for God that is reclaiming lives from the kingdom
of darkness must also expect attacks from the enemy.[12]

A Generation Under Attack

World Vision's Bryant Myers contends that unseen forces are
not only at work at street level, but to be discerned in the institutions behind some of the economic and social conditions
which push and pull children away from their homes and families and onto the streets.

The kind of largescale change needed to successfully deal
with issues like street children cannot be delivered by secular
society, he maintains, for 'this kind of change does not come
from laws or even economic incentives'.[13]

He went on: 'It comes from another source altogether—a
source that can change hearts of stone, that has the authority
to drive the demonic from the corridors of power, and from
the comfortable offices of the marketplace.'

His observations are echoed by urban missions specialist
Roger Greenaway, who sees action by decisionmakers as well
as at street level to be vital.

'These urban armies of desperate children are symptoms of
a whole network of problems that are social and economic,
religious and political, familial and personal in nature,' he
reflected.[14]

Rounding up children and keeping them out of sight for a
while does nothing to solve the cancerous problems that forced
them onto the streets in the first place.

Without question, far-reaching and highly inter-related solutions have to be found that will reorder urban life at all levels. That is what urban mission is all about.

Missionary for a quarter of a century, Dean Sherman, a noted Bible teacher on spiritual warfare, believes that children are Satan's prime target for his war with God.

'It is easy to see throughout history and today that Satan zealously targets children, seeking their bondage and destruction,' he says.[15] 'The enmity between children and the enemy is especially strong.

'Children are new and innocent, the "seed of woman"'— between the Devil and whom, God said after the Fall, there would be contention.[16] 'From the fires of Moloch in Old Testament times, where parents sacrificed newborn babies on the red-hot arms of idols; to present-day war atrocities, abortion, drug addiction, and child pornography; children are under direct attack from Satan.'[17]

New Zealand youth specialist and Bible teacher Winkie Pratney sees a similar demonic plot behind the headlines, citing the growing number of runaway and abandoned youngsters on the streets of Western cities as one indicator.

Together with the rise in abortions and teen suicides, he sees a new 'contract' out on children, like those issued when babies and newborns were killed in the early days of the lives of Moses and Jesus.[18]

Then, 'that rage missed its marks. The targets of that destruction each time escaped. And the ones that got away did untold damage to hell's kingdom', he notes, concluding:

There is something precious and important about this generation, so deeply under attack . . . It may have among its ranks of survivors the makings of a major spiritual miracle. There may be leaders-to-be rescued from the sword and the burning altars of Moloch that will lead an entire generation of the abandoned, loveless and lonely into the promises of God.[19]

REACHING OUT

'Simply . . . regaining for him
the inheritance of which . . .
he has been fraudulently deprived.'

OLIVER TWIST: CHAPTER FORTY-ONE

LOOKING BACK ON the months of interviews and research, could there not have been easier ways to tackle this subject?

Perhaps just pick one country, one city, one centre and tell some of the stories of the kids and the workers.

But that might have made it too easy for us to have read and moved on; after all, that was just 'there', wasn't it?

Hopefully the preceding pages have, instead, persuaded you that street children are a global issue, a world concern.

Which means we all have a responsibility.

The danger of just focusing on one 'story', too, is that it would be easy to turn it more into a kind of street-level soap opera.

Similarly, the attempt has been made to make sure that this book is not just a string of sensational stories—several shocking ones were deliberately omitted—that produce a sense of pity.

As a human feeling it only goes so far, and centres more on our reaction to what we have experienced than the subjects concerned. It is more about us than them.

Rather, the hope is that this brief 'world tour' combines a sense of the big picture with some of the small details in such a way that it may elicit compassion.

That is, pity with feet on it. Feelings that go somewhere.

The first chapter of Mark's gospel tells the story of the leper who came to Jesus and asked Him to make him clean.

Verse 41 tells how 'Filled with compassion, Jesus *reached out* . . .'

So what can you do in response to the needs of the world's millions of street children?

First, you have already done something. Thank you!

By buying (hopefully!) this book, you have made a contribution: a portion of the sale price, and all author royalties from each copy will go to support street children ministries and organisations.

If you would like details on how author royalties are distributed each year, please send a self-addressed envelope to:

Andy Butcher
PO Box 26479, Colorado Springs,
CO 80936, USA

Hopefully, too, you have been awakened not only to a human problem, but to a divine solution.

It is one that you can help implement.

You can be part of God's plan to regain their fraudulently deprived inheritance as you:

- PRAY for the street children of the world.

  Perhaps isolate a particular country or even city. Pray, too, for the agencies and organisations working there.

- GIVE to the ministries that are working for street children, either directly in hands-on help, or behind the scenes in advocacy and information. Or both. Some contact addresses are in this book.

- GO yourself and find out more. Maybe there is an urban ministry you can volunteer time to in your city or region. Several overseas ministries welcome short-term help, too.

  Perhaps through this involvement you may feel called to full-time service!

- WATCH for news about street children on TV and in the newspapers. Write to elected representatives, embassies and other agencies as appropriate to express your concern.

Don't just do it all alone, though. Remember there is mutual support or encouragement in a group.

Draw a group of friends together from your church or neighbourhood and form a Street Children Action Group. Together you could:

- ADOPT a country, city, or ministry and support them through prayer and finances.

- RAISE awareness in your church and community through information events, exhibitions and letters/articles to the local media.

Responding to the need will also mean dispelling some myths. In the same way that Dicken's *Oliver Twist* has been romanticised, it is easy to have too simple a view of a complex issue.

As Jesus urged His first disciples when He sent them out on an early ministry trip, so we present-day Christians should always be innocent, never naïve.[1]

We need to separate what is wrong from what is simply different to our experience and understanding.

For Christians that will mean understanding justice from God's perspective, discerning not so much just the human rights as the biblical rights.

For example, to many Western minds, the idea of having no roof to sleep under at night is appalling. Yet in parts of the tropical, developing world it can be the most comfortable place to be.

So being 'on the street' may not, in itself, be a bad thing. What is the real issue is the environment in which the young person finds him- or herself.

They may not necessarily so much need rescuing from the streets as safeguarding while they are there, protected from exploitation and provided for.

As Stefan Vanistandael, deputy secretary-general of the International Catholic Child Bureau which has promoted church-based initiatives for street children, notes, they are often referred to as a 'problem'.

But where, actually, he asks, is the real problem?

It may be argued that street children are children who try to survive with much intelligence and skill in very difficult circumstances.

Some people may find them a nuisance, but street children may find adults a nuisance. Precisely because they are children, it is hard to pretend that they are responsible for the situation in which they have to survive.

At most, their presence is a symptom of a disease. It is not the disease itself.[2]

As with cancer, that means doing everything possible to help those who are suffering now, while working hard to develop a cure—reaching the young ones at street level, and seeking to change the social and economic problems that can force them there.

It will be a slow business. Countries crippled by debt or without moral foundations cannot be rebuilt overnight.

And it often takes more than a bath and a quick prayer to restore a childhood old before its time.

But it can happen. It does happen. It should happen.

The last words belong to Oliver.

His inheritance restored, he journeys to his new home, and remembers a young friend left behind.

'It will make you cry, I know, to hear what he can tell,' he says to his benefactors,[3] 'but never mind, never mind, it will all be over, and you will smile again—I know that too—to think how changed he is; you did the same with me . . .'

May it be true for his 'descendants' around the world today—the *scugnizzo* (spinning tops) of Italy; the *pajaro frutero* (fruit birds) of Peru; the *moustiques* (mosquitoes) of Cameroon; the *desechables* (throwaways) of Colombia.

Or Zaire's *moineaux* (sparrows), which, the Psalmist declared, even found a place of refuge close to God.[4]

And not one of which, Jesus assured His followers, was forgotten by Him.[5]

Who Will Save The Children?

by Randy Stonehill

Cry for all the innocent ones
Born into a world that's lost its heart
For those who never learn to dream
Because their hope is crushed before they can start
And we shake our fists at the air
And say, 'If God is love, how can this be fair?'

But we are His hands
We are His voice
We are the ones who must make the choice
And if it isn't now, tell me when?
If it isn't you, then tell me
Who will save the children?
Who will save the children?

We count our blessings one by one
Yet we have forgotten how to give
It seems that we don't want to face
All the hungry and homeless who struggle to live
But heaven is watching tonight
Tugging at our hearts to do what's right

And we are His hands
We are His voice
We are the ones who must make the choice
And if it isn't now, tell me when?
If it isn't you, then tell me

Street Children

Who will save the children?
Who will save the children?

As we observe them through our TV screens
They seem so distant and unreal
But they bleed like we bleed
And they feel what we feel
Oh, save the children
Save the children

Now we decide that nothing can change
And throw up our hands in numb despair
And we lose a piece of our souls
By teaching ourselves just how not to care
But Christ would have gone to the Cross
Just to save one child from being lost

And we are His hands
We are His voice
We are the ones who must make the choice
And it must be now
There's no time to lose
It must be you
No one can take your place
Can't you see that only we can
Save the children
Save the children
Save the children
Please, save the children

From the album *Celebrate This Heartbeat* (Word Inc, 1984). Words and music by Randy Stonehill. Reproduced with permission.

RESOURCES

Recommended further reading

Street Children: A growing urban tragedy
by Susanna Agnelli (Wiedenfeld)
—Mid-1980s overview report by committee of the Independent Commission on International Humani-tarian Issues

Street Children of Cali
by Lewis Aptekar (Duke University Press, USA)
—One of the most detailed surveys of street children to date, centring on one Colombian city

Malunde: The street children of Hillbrow
by Jill Swart (University of South Africa)
—Well researched, more accessible study of street children of Johannesburg

The Next Generation: Lives of Third World children
by Judith Ennew and Brian Milne (Zed Books)
—Wide-ranging review of the social and economic issues affecting and facing children in the developing world

Stolen Childhood
by Anuradha Vittachi (Polity Press)
—Companion to acclaimed TV series on child abuse, labour and poverty

Brazil: War on children
by Gilberto Dimenstein (Latin America Bureau)
—Disturbing investigation by Brazilian journalist of the truth behind the 'death squad' headlines

Companion to the Poor
by Viv Grigg (MARC)
—Christian perspective on missions among the poor and needy

Urban Children in Distress
edited by Cristina Szanton Blanc (UNICEF)
—Thorough examination of the street level and broader social issues, plus discussion of effectness of current initiatives, focusing on Brazil, the Philippines, India, Kenya and Italy

Crisis on the Streets: a manual for ministry to street children
(ACTION International)
—Practical 'how to' manual for churches/groups contemplating street children's ministry

Oliver Twist
by Charles Dickens
—Classic novelisation of the birth of modern-day street children

Street Children International Directory
(Dorcas Aid, see p.205)
—Guide to many of the Christian ministries working among street children around the world

Healing the Children of War
edited by Phyllis Kilbourn (MARC Books, USA)
—Practical manual by professionals working with child victims, covering topics such as recognising troubled children, how to give comfort and restore hope.

Forthcoming in 1996:

Street Smarts: A handbook for ministry to street children (MARC)
edited by Phyllis Kilbourn (MARC Books, USA)
—Articles from the 'experts', aimed at those involved professionally with street children

For children and teenagers:

Carlos: The street boy who found a home
by Marcos Carpenter (Children Around the World series, by Eerdmans)
—Simple, effective picture-storybook of youngster saved from the streets

Street Boy
by Fletch Brown (ACTION International, see p. 205)
—Fictionalised account of ministry to street children, in the Philippines, through the eyes of a shoeshine boy who becomes a Christian at an evangelistic camp

The Bandit of Ashley Downs by Dave and Neta Jackson
(Trailblazer Books series by Bethany House Publishers, USA)

—Fictionalised account of George Müller's pioneering ministry among abandoned children

Streetlife—An educational resource for secondary schools about street children (Jubilee Action)
—Excellent classroom discussion/activity materials

Recommended further viewing

Salaam Bombay! (Mirabal Films)
—Award-winning drama about lives of street children of Bombay, shot entirely on location with key roles filled by real-life street kids. Available on video rental.

Pixote
—Earliest attempt to bring the dangerous world of street children to the screen. Slightly dated now, but still effective. Portuguese, subtitled. Available on video rental.

Streetwise
—Gritty, disturbing black-and-white picture of lives of group of young teens on the streets of Seattle, USA. Part-drama, part-documentary. Available on video rental.

Missing
—Evangelistic/missions family-viewing drama about street boy in Manila. Available with discussion materials on church loan from Gospel Films, 2735 East Apple Avenue, Muskegon, MI 49442, USA.

Organisations supporting street children projects include:

TEAR Fund
100 Church Road
Teddington
Middlesex TW11 8QE
UK

World Vision UK
599 Avebury Boulevard
Central Milton Keynes
Buckinghamshire MK9 3PG
UK

Christian Aid
PO Box 100
London SE1 7RT
UK

Dorcas Aid
PO Box 12
1619 ZG Andijk
The Netherlands

Christmas Cracker
PO Box 43
Sutton
Surrey SM2 5WL
UK

Save the Children Fund
Mary Datchelor House
17 Grove Lane
London SE5 8RD
UK

Compassion International
PO Box 7000
Colorado Springs
CO 80933
USA

Pan de Vida
AA 052320
114 Santafe de Bogota, 2
Colombia
South America

Viva
PO Box 633
Oxford
OX2 0NS

Jubilee Action
St Johns, Cranleigh Road
Wonersh, Guildford
Surrey GU5 0QX
UK

Groups working directly with street children include:

Youth With A Mission
(in various countries)
13 Highfield Oval
Ambrose Lane
Harpenden
Herts AL5 4BX
UK

ACTION International
(in various countries)
PO Box 490
Bothell
WA 98041-0409
USA

Research and campaign organisations include:

UNICEF UK
55 Lincoln's Inn Fields
London WC2 3NB
UK

Amnesty International
1 Easton Street
London WC1X 8DJ
UK

Jubilee Action
(see previous entry)

Viva
(see previous entry)

International Catholic
    Child Bureau
65 rue de Lausanne
1202 Geneva
Switzerland

Childhope UK
44 Roseberry Avenue
London EC1R 4RN
UK

NOTES

Chapter Two: Saving Trees, Dying Children

1. *World Declaration on the Survival, Protection and Development of Children* (United Nations, 1990)
2. Personal correspondence with James Beanaux, children's worker (1991)
3. Personal newsletter of Johan and Jeannette Lukasse, children's workers (1989)
4. *Young Runaways Case Study* by The Children's Society, 1992
5. *World Declaration* (see note 1)
6. Ibid.
7. Ibid.
8. 'The Children's Summit', *Newsweek*, 1 October 1990
9. Plan of Action for Implementing the *World Declaration on the Survival, Protection and Development of Children* (United Nations, 1990)
10. *World Summit for Children: Words and images* (UNICEF, 1990)
11. 'Talk of the Town' column in *The New Yorker*, 29 June 1992
12. Daniel McGrory, 'They shoot children, don't they?' *The Daily Express*, 18 May 1992
13. Caroline Moorhead (ed.), *Betrayal* (Doubleday, 1990)
14. Ibid.
15. *Children's Rights Need International Protection* (United Nations Centre for Human Rights and UNICEF, 1991)
16. Ibid.
17. UNICEF Information Kit for World Summit for Children.
18. Maxine Shideler, 'UN Convention on the Rights of the Child gives State ultimate control over children', *Colorado Christian News*, March 1995
19. Jasmine Birtles, 'On the streets of Europe', *Time and Tide* magazine, 1990
20. Associated Press report, June 1994
21. 'Homeless in Moscow', *Pulse* magazine (Evangelical Missions Information Service, September 1994)
22. 'Abandoned Children, the Most Marginalised', *Together* (World Vision International Journal), October–December 1991)

23. 'Children of the Gutter', *Newsweek,* 1 May 1989
24. *Children Without Families* (Save the Children Fund, 1988)
25. *Together* (see note 21)
26. Annual statistical table on global mission: 1994 (*International Bulletin of Missionary Research,* January/February 1994)
27. Ibid.
28. *Cities of Children: The child cannot wait...* (The Panos Institute, 1990)
29. Anuradha Vittachi, *Stolen Childhood* (Polity Press, 1989)

Chapter Three: From Crusade to Revolution
1. Genesis 4
2. Genesis 4:12
3. Judith Ennew and Brian Milne, *The Next Generation: Lives of Third World children* (Zed Books, 1989)
4. John Boswell, *The Kindness of Strangers: The abandonment of children in Western Europe from late antiquity to the Renaissance* (Pantheon, 1988)
5. Ibid.
6. C. John Sommerville, *The Rise and Fall of Childhood* (Vintage, 1990)
7. George Zabriskie Gray, *The Children's Crusade: A history* (1870; republished by William Morrow & Co, 1972)
8. Ibid.
9. *Encyclopaedia of World Problems and Human Potential* (Union of International Associations, 1994)
10. Moorhead, *Betrayal* (see note 13, chapter 2)
11. Norman Page, *A Dickens Companion* (MacMillan Press, 1984)
12. Victor Hugo, *Les Miserables*
13. 'Kids' horror is winning awards', Parentguide supplement in *Parentwise,* October 1994
14. Ibid.
15. Robert H. Bremmer (ed.), *Children and Youth in America: A documentary history* (Harvard University Press, 1970)
16. Charles Loring Brace, *The Best Method of Disposing of Our Pauper and Vagrant Children* (Wynkoop, Hallenback & Thomas, 1859)
17. *The Life of Charles Loring Brace Chiefly Told in His Own Letters,*

edited by his daughter (Charles Scribner & Sons, 1894)

18. A. E. Williams, *Barnardo of Stepney* (Guild Books, 1953)
19. Ibid.
20. Eileen Simpson, *Orphans—Real and Imaginary* (Weidenfeld & Nicolson, 1987)
21. Ennew and Milne, *The Next Generation* (see note 3)
22. Jo Boyden with Pat Holden, *Children of the Cities* (Zed Books, 1991)
23. Ennew and Milne, *The Next Generation* (see note 3)
24. *Street Children: a growing urban tragedy*—report for the Independent Commission on International Humanitarian Issues, presented by Susanna Agnelli (Weidenfeld & Nicolson, 1986)
25. Ibid.

Chapter Four: Streetwise and Stressed

1. Lewis Aptekar, *Street Children of Cali* (Duke University Press, 1988)
2. Ibid.
3. Ibid.
4. Ibid.
5. *Children on Jakarta's Streets* (Childhope, 1991)
6. Ibid.
7. *In the Streets: Working street children in Asuncion* (UNICEF, 1988)
8. Ibid.
9. *The Situation of Street Children in Ten Cities,* (Joint Department of Social Welfare, National Council of Social Development of the Philippines, and UNICEF Project 1988)
10. Proceedings of the First Metro Manila Street Children's Conference (National Council of Social Development Foundation, 1990)
11. Ellen Switzer, *Anyplace But Here* (Atheneum, 1992)
12. Patricia Connors with Dorianne Perrucci, *Runaways: Coping at home and on the street* (Rosen Publishing, 1989)
13. 'A Call for Action', press release by The Children's Society, March 1992
14. Mike Stein, Gwyther Rees and Nick Frost, *Running the Risk: Young people on the streets of Britain today* (The Children's Society, 1994)
15. Interviewed in Angela Neustatter, 'With one foot in the gutter', *The Guardian,* 16 December 1987

16. Boyden with Holden, *Children of the Cities* (see note 22, chapter 3)
17. Childhope UK pamphlet (1991)

Chapter Five: The Killing Grounds
 1. *Jubilee Action,* newsletter 19 (Jubilee Campaign, 1990)
 2. Associated Press report, 24 July 1993
 3. *Jubilee Action* (see note 1)
 4. *Violence Against Children and Adolescents in Brazil—Trends and perspectives* (unofficial translation) by the National Commission to Combat Violence Against Children and Adolescents (Ministry of Justice Human Rights Commission, 1992)
 5. *The Killing of Children and Adolescents in Brazil,* report by the Centre for the Mobilisation of Marginalised Populations (1988)
 6. Gilberto Dimenstein, *Brazil: War on children* (Latin America Bureau, 1991)
 7. *World Report 1990* (Human Rights Watch)
 8. Dimenstein, *Brazil* (see note 6)
 9. Ibid.
10. McGrory, 'They shoot children, don't they?' (see note 12, chapter 2)
11. *Street Children: Guatemala and Brazil report* (Jubilee Campaign, 1992)
12. Ibid.
13. Caroline Moorhead, 'Torture and jail for boys in Guatemala', *The Independent,* October 1990
14. *Guatemala: Amnesty International's current human rights concerns* (Amnesty International, 1991)
15. Timothy Ross, 'Children of a lesser god?' *BBC Worldwide,* December 1993
16. Ibid.
17. Jubilee Action news release (5 October, 1994)
18. *Street Children in Colombia,* report by Jubilee Action (1994)
19. Philippines Campaign Press Conference, Jubilee Campaign, 1992
20. 'Colombia—crusading efforts bring signs of progress', *Aidswatch* (Panoscope, 1990)
21. Marguerite Michaels, 'Rio's dead-end kids', *Time* magazine, 9 August 1993
22. Dimenstein, *Brazil* (see note 6)
23. Ibid.

24. Moorhead, *Betrayal* (see note 13, chapter 2)
25. Dimenstein, *Brazil* (see note 6)
26. Marilyn Rocky, *Whose Child Was This?* (Childhope USA, 1991)
27. *Street Children: Guatemala and Brazil report* (see note 11)
28. *Frontline: Children of the night* (WGBH Educational Foundation, 1989)

Chapter Six: Bodies for Sale

1. *The Street Girls of Metro Manila: Vulnerable victims of today's silent wars* (Childhope, 1989)
2. Ibid.
3. *The Situation of Street Children in Ten Cities* (see note 9, chapter 4)
4. Ibid.
5. Ron O'Grady, *Children Worldwide: An international campaign against sex tourism* (International Catholic Child Bureau, 1992)
6. Cristina Szanton Blanc (ed.), *Urban Children in Distress* (UNICEF, 1994)
7. Ron O'Grady, *The Child and the Tourist* (ECPAT, 1992)
8. *Street Children in the Philippines,* report by Jubilee Campaign, 1992
9. Ibid.
10. Peter Lee-Wright, *Child Slaves* (Earthscan Publications, 1990)
11. Sister Mary Rose McGeady, *Am I Going to Heaven?* (Covenant House, 1994)
12. 'AIDS: A growing threat to street children' (Childhope, October 1990)
13. McGrory, 'They shoot children, don't they?'(see note 12, chapter 2)
14. Personal newsletter of Johan and Jeannette Lukasse (December 1992)
15. From his chapter in *Protecting Working Children,* edited by William E. Myers (Zed Books, 1991)
16. Ibid.
17. *Children on Jakarta's Streets* (see note 5, chapter 4)
18. Charles Sow, 'Senegal's *talibes*: Begging for God or greed?' *Together,* April–June 1994
19. Ibid.
20. *Institute of Psychological and Educational Research Project on Child Labour: a brief report*

21. 'Trafficking in Children for Adoption', chapter in Moorhead (ed.), *Betrayal* (see note 13, chapter 2)
22. *IDEA* (magazine of The Evangelical Alliance, UK) 1993
23. Ibid.

Chapter Seven: The Missing Mission

1. Personal interview, Colorado Springs, USA, September 1992
2. 'The world's street children need to be reached with the gospel of Jesus Christ', *City Watch*, 1993
3. John R. Cheyne, 'Street Children: A new frontier', *The Commission*, (Foreign Mission Board of Southern Baptist Convention, April 1993)
4. Wesley Stafford, 'Making children matter in the Great Commission', *Compassion* magazine, Autumn 1994
5. Bryant L. Myers, 'State of the World's Children: Critical challenge to Christian mission', *International Bulletin of Missionary Research*, July 1994
6. Galatians 3:28
7. 'The rehabilitation of street children: case studies from Manila', *City Watch* (Institute of Global Urban Studies Autumn 1993)
8. 'Hindrances to street kid workers', *City Watch—Asia* (Institute of Global Urban Studies, 1992)

Chapter Eight: 'The Children of China' Choise

1. Personal interview, Amsterdam 1991
2. *A Million and a Half in Answer to Prayer: Autobiography of George Müller* (J. Nesbit & Co, 1914)
3. Ibid.
4. Dr A. T. Pierson, *George Müller of Bristol* (Pickering & Inglis, 1949)
5. *A Million and a Half in Answer to Prayer* (see note 2)
6. Williams, *Barnardo of Stepney* (see note 18, chapter 3)
7. Ibid.
8. John Woodbridge (ed.), *More Than Conquerors* (Moody Press, 1993)
9. Ibid.
10. Richard Collier, *The General Next to God* (Collins, 1965)
11. *The Life of Charles Loring Brace* (see note 17, chapter 3)
12. Ibid.

13. Marilyn Holt, *The Orphan Trains* (University of Michigan, 1992)
14. Louis de Wohl, *Founded on a Rock: A history of the Catholic Church* (Lippincott, 1961)
15. Ronda De Sola Chervin, *Quotable Saints* (Servant Publications, 1992)
16. David L. Edwards, *Christian England* (revised edition) (Fount, 1988)
17. Ruth Tucker and Walter Liedefeld, *Daughters of the Church* (Academie Books, 1987)
18. Monica Whiting, 'Knowing when your work is done', *Compassion* magazine, September/October 1993
19. Diana Garland, *Precious in His Sight: A guide to child advocacy* (New Hope, 1993)
20. Ibid.

Chapter Nine: 'Don't Lose the Little Ones'

1. Matthew 18:1
2. Matthew 20:20–27; Mark 10:35–45
3. John 12:49–50; John 5:19
4. Matthew 18:3
5. Matthew 18:6
6. *The Rise and Fall of Childhood* (see note 6, chapter 3)
7. Ibid.
8. Matthew 18:10
9. Ibid.
10. Psalm 91:11
11. Luke 15:1–7
12. Matthew 18:14
13. Matthew 22:1–14; Luke 14:15–24
14. Mark 10:14
15. Ibid.
16. Mark 10:16
17. Luke 4:18–21
18. Mark 14:7
19. Ibid.
20. Deuteronomy 15:4–5
21. James 1:27
22. Matthew 5:17
23. Exodus 22:22–24

24. Deuteronomy 10:18
25. Deuteronomy 24:19–21
26. Deuteronomy 26:12
27. Deuteronomy 27:19
28. Job 29:11–12, 16
29. Job 1:8
30. Job 31:16–22
31. Psalm 10:14, 18
32. Psalm 68:5
33. Psalm 94:5–6
34. Psalm 146:7, 9
35. Genesis 18:20
36. Ezekiel 16:49
37. Ezekiel 16:50
38. Isaiah 1:5
39. Isaiah 1:16–17
40. Jeremiah 5:28
41. Jeremiah 7:5–7
42. Mark 16:15
43. Colossians 1:27–28
44. 'The world's street children need to be reached . . .' (see note 2, chapter 7)
45. 'State of the World's Children' (see note 5, chapter 7)
46. 'The rehabilitation of street children' (see note 6, chapter 7)
47. Ibid.

Chapter Ten: The Rescuers
1. Gordon Aeschliman, *Global Trends* (IVP, 1990)
2. Gustavo Gorritt, 'Saviour of the street children', *Reader's Digest*, June 1992
3. 'Pornography: A victimless crime?', *World* magazine, January 1994
4. 'Former porn star fighting back', *Movieguide*, May 1994
5. Nat Belz and Michael Cromartie, 'This one thing I do', *World* magazine, December 1993

Chapter Eleven: When Love Breaks Through
1. 'A street kid who made it' in *City Watch* (Institute of Global Urban Studies, Autumn 1994)
2. Ibid.

3. 'The rehabilitation of street children' (see note 7, chapter 7)
4. Ibid.
5. ACTION Street Children newsletter (1992)

Chapter Twelve: The Tug of War
1. Charles Dickens, *Oliver Twist* (chapter 34)
2. Ibid.
3. Ibid.
4. Angus Wilson in Introduction to *Oliver Twist*, ed. Peter Fairclough (Penguin Classic, 1985)
5. Ibid.
6. Ibid.
7. Antoinette Galbraith, 'Streetwise', *Woman Alive!*, September 1994
8. Jenny Taylor, 'Beggars belief ', *21CC* magazine, August 1989
9. Patrick McDonald, *Street Kids in the Latin Americas* (Viva Foundation, 1993)
10. Street children's research project report for selected areas of Metro Manila (ACTION International Ministries, 1992)
11. Ibid.
12. Provincial Home Study Report (ACTION International Ministries, 1992)
13. 'State of the World's Children' (see note 5, chapter 7)
14. Roger Greenaway (ed.), *Discipling the City* (Baker Books, 1992)
15. Dean Sherman, *Spiritual Warfare for Every Christian* (Youth With A Mission Publishing, 1990)
16. Genesis 3:15
17. Sherman, *Spiritual Warfare* (see note 15)
18. Winkie Pratney, *Devil Take the Youngest: The war on childhood* (Huntington House, 1985)
19. Ibid.

Afterword: Reaching Out
1. Matthew 10:16
2. Stefan Vanistendael, *Street Children: An overview* (International Catholic Child Bureau, 1990)
3. *Oliver Twist*, chapter 51
4. Psalm 84:3
5. Luke 12:6